PADUCAH

FRONTIER TO THE ATOMIC AGE

At the turn of the twentieth century, Mayor James Smith entertained at "Bide-a-Wee," his home at the edge of Paducah, which now serves as the Kentucky Welcome Center.

Cover: Employees of Jackson Foundry pose for this portrait. (JSJ.)

THE
MAKING OF AMERICA
SERIES

PADUCAH

FRONTIER TO THE ATOMIC AGE

JOHN E.L. ROBERTSON

ARCADIA
PUBLISHING

ISBN 978-0-7385-2376-7

Published by Arcadia Publishing,
Charleston, South Carolina

Printed in the United States of America

Library of Congress Control Number: 2002100894

For all general information contact Arcadia Publishing at:
Telephone 843-853-2070
Fax 843-853-0044
E-mail sales@arcadiapublishing.com
For customer service and orders:
Toll-Free 1-888-313-2665

Visit us on the Internet at www.arcadiapublishing.com

Will Jackson and friends pose in front of the Richmond House Hotel. (Courtesy JSJ.)

Contents

ACKNOWLEDGMENTS

Thanks to those at the Paducah Tourist Bureau, the William Clark Museum, the Filson Club, the U.S. Navy Museum, the Kentucky Historical Society, various librarians, and especially Joseph Donnelly in Jersey City, New Jersey, and to Vonnie Shelton at the McCracken County, Kentucky Library, and to all other libraries consulted for courteous assistance beyond the norm. Many shared their pictures and my thanks are offered, especially to J.S. Jackson, Robert and Jack Johnston, the families of Vic Meredith, Dr. William Blalock, and Glenn Schrader, and to the Canadian National–Illinois Central Railroad.

Most historians profess a love for the Muse Clio; I reserve mine for Margaret and all my family.

ABBREVIATIONS

The images that appear in this book were provided by a number of organizations and individuals. Credit for these images is provided at the end of captions and some are abbreviated as follows:

JSJ	J.S. Jackson
JJ	Jack Johnston
McCPL	McCracken County Public Library
MHM	Market House Museum
SB	Steve Birchfield

INTRODUCTION

From pleasure to pathos, Paducah is a microcosm for peering into the past. One of the last frontier communities east of the Mississippi River, the community came late but advanced rapidly. During the Civil War, Paducah took part in Kentucky's futile effort to remain neutral. When the state was invaded by the Confederacy, General U.S. Grant made his first independent decision of the war by seizing Paducah, forcing the state to commit itself to the Union. Citizens in the city continued to hold an independent view, much to the dismay of the Union occupiers. When Grant expelled all Jews from the territory under his command, Paducah Jews protested to President Lincoln, who rescinded the order. When rebel forces raided the city twice in 1864, General E.A. Paine sought to squelch Southern sympathy. Citizens from Paducah favoring the South were expelled to Canada.

Long the entertainment center for the western part of Kentucky, Paducah continues to expand its role in this area. Recently it exchanged visits with its boys' choir and Vienna's. Paducah also sports a symphony orchestra and chorus, making it an island of classical music near the core of country music in Nashville.

Sports fascinate Paducahans. The Indians were Paducah's professional baseball team in the Kitty League. The Augusta Tilghman High School teams once played against Little Rock, Arkansas, and other powerhouses in the middle of America. Clarence Gains, the third winningest college basketball coach in America, is from Paducah, and the junior college in Paducah won the NJCAA basketball championship in 1969.

Race relations run the gamut from a lynching in 1916 to the city becoming one of the test cases that led to national integration. African-American Paducahans such as William Nelsen and W.G. Harvey made significant contributions to state and nation.

In politics, Alben Barkley left an indelible mark on both the U.S. Senate and the modern office of vice president. He also made "the Veep" a national title. "Dolly" McNutt was the first woman in Kentucky to become the mayor of a second-class city. Early on, Paducah learned to listen and use the skills and expertise of its citizens.

Paducah continues to reinvent itself. Its central location on major transportation systems such as the inland waterway promises a future with the opportunity to play a major role in the history of the nation.

1. BEGINNINGS

The site that is now Paducah, Kentucky, came to the attention of George Rogers Clark in 1778 while he was en route to capture the former French towns in the Illinois country along the lower Ohio River during the American Revolution. With few men and scant supplies, Clark left the Redstone settlement near present Pittsburgh in early May with about 150 men bound for the Falls of the Ohio (now Louisville). In his secret orders to Clark, Virginia Governor Patrick Henry extended him the authority to seize any British forts he deemed advisable. Low water forced Clark to stop at the falls, where he drilled his troops. While on an island there, Clark planted a corn crop to cover a retreat if that should be needed later in the summer.

Proceeding down the river, the party camped on the north (Illinois) side just above the mouth of the Tennessee. While there, Clark noted that the land on the opposite shore at the mouth of the Tennessee gave promise as a city site; however, other affairs were at hand. He proceeded west, stopped short of the mouth of the Ohio to fool the French and Indians of the area who were watching for him, and marched overland from Massac Creek to Kaskaskia, where the fort and town were taken without a casualty. Thus, Clark began his conquest of more territory from the British than any other single person during the Revolution. His exploits gave Clark and the state of Virginia, his sponsor, claim to the entire Northwest Territory, which encompassed all lands east of the Mississippi, north of the Ohio, and south of the Great Lakes eastward to the Appalachian Mountains.

George Rogers Clark did not live to see the town he envisioned come to pass, but he did get a Virginia treasury warrant and he did lay claim to the Paducah site in 1795. Nothing more could be done until the Chickasaw claim to extensive tracts in Kentucky and Tennessee was extinguished.

In 1818, Isaac Shelby and Andrew Jackson agreed to act on behalf of the United States in negotiating a treaty with the Chickasaw that required them to cede their claim to all lands in Kentucky and Tennessee lying west of the Tennessee River. This region now is called "The Jackson Purchase" despite the fact that the Kentucky delegate, Isaac Shelby, was senior. His illness at the time required Jackson to do most of the actual negotiating. At loose ends after his ouster from the army, Jackson joined other Tennessee speculators in a grab for promising land along the Mississippi River. His treatment of the Chickasaw during the negotiations was harsh. Also, the United States in 1805 had promised

This statue of George Rogers Clark stands in Fort Massac State Park in Metropolis, Illinois. Clark first saw the mouth of the Tennessee River in 1778 and laid a claim to the site of Paducah in 1795; however, he was unable to found a town due to debt and the hostility of the Chickasaw, who also claimed all of Kentucky and Tennessee west of the Cumberland River until the treaties of 1805 and 1818.

the Chickasaw by treaty that they would not have to cede more of their land "as long as the sun shines and the grass grows."

Clark died before the Senate ratified the treaty allowing settlement at the mouth of the Tennessee River. Because Clark was deeply in debt, his claim to that point had gone to his younger brother William (of Lewis and Clark fame); however, the claim was later disputed. The courts disallowed the deed, claiming it was "fraudulent as to the creditors of George Rogers Clark." At Clark's death in 1818, the estate owed 535 pounds, 3 shillings, and 5 pence.

Court records show that William Clark tried to purchase the site of Paducah. However, this transaction later was found to be defective, so the court corrected the record to show that George Woolfolk of Shelbyville, Kentucky (a friend of the court), purchased the land. The heirs of George Rogers Clark were instructed to deed the land to Woolfolk, and if they failed to do so, Samuel Dickinson, as the court appointed commissioner, was ordered "to do it for them." The heirs did nothing. Dickinson acted on June 16, 1827. Woolfolk later sold the land to William Clark on October 13, 1827, for "the sum of five dollars in hand paid." (This event is commemorated in Paducah by a historical marker.)

William Clark had to fend off still another and more grievous threat to his claim. In the normal course of things, Virginia gave preference to military claims and then to treasury warrants. When Kentucky separated from Virginia in 1791, all Virginia land grants were to be honored. The estate of Colonel Charles Porterfield, killed during the Revolution at the Battle of Camden, South Carolina, claimed the same site as William Clark in 1824, 1825, and 1826, using a military warrant of Virginia, claiming it took precedence over the earlier Clark treasury warrant claim. This dispute went to the Supreme Court in its 1844 Porterfield

Script case, in which the earlier claim of the Clarks was affirmed. Before Clark's claim was final, however, settlement began and the town was named.

On April 27, 1827, William Clark wrote a letter to his son Meriwether Lewis Clark, a cadet at West Point. Clark told his son that he was leaving St. Louis for the mouth of the Tennessee River on the twenty-sixth of May where he planned to lay out a town. William wrote that he named the town in remembrance of a proud tribe "once the largest nation of Indians known in this country, and now almost forgotten." This tribe was located near the Red River in what is now Texas when Clark heard of them. Once numerous, they had been debased by contact with Europeans to the point of slavery and extermination. William wished to perpetuate the memory of this people and made certain that future generations would know how the name would be pronounced by changing the spelling from the French *Padouca* to "Pa-du-cah."

Communities frequently reinvent themselves. Paducah is the only major city in Kentucky that bears an Indian name. Clark's account of the derivation of the city's name seems simple enough. Why, then, does a legend persist claiming the town was named for a heroic giant, the chieftain of a sub-tribe of the Chickasaw, named Paduke? According to this tale, Clark was to meet this ancient friend at the mouth of the Tennessee in 1818; however, the old Indian died along the way. The town accepted this legend and amplified it over time. Several theories existed, but according to Fred Neuman in *Paducahans in History*, "one . . . is the doctrine that in the olden time an Indian chief was buried on the banks of the Tennessee. . . . The romance that surrounds this hypothesis will not be willingly sacrificed by the average Paducahian." Neuman further amplified the legend in "Chief Paduke and His Peaceful Indian Tribe" complete with fanciful names and characteristics. The chief grows in stature and nobility with each retelling.

William Clark founded Paducah after returning from his trek with Meriwether Lewis and the Corps of Discover, which penetrated the wilderness to the Pacific between 1803 and 1806.

The statue of legendary Chief Paduke was created by sculptor Lorado Taft.

The local chapter of the Daughters of the American Revolution commissioned a statue of the chief by Lorado Taft of Chicago in 1909. This monument dedicated to the memory of the icon now stands at the intersection of Jefferson Street and Nineteenth. Moreover, the official seal of the city sports a stylized replica of the warrior. By 1913, locals were delighted to welcome the arrival of the legendary chieftain (played by James Wheeler) at the waterfront as a part of the homecoming celebration of the city.

A catalyst for confrontation between Paducah and other cities was a speech by Kenneth M. Bradley, president of Chicago's Bush Conservatory of Music and Dramatic Arts, given in Louisville on March 3, 1916. Bradley repeated what he remembered sculptor Taft saying about the statue during a civic club luncheon in Chicago, to the effect that it did not portray a particular person but was a representation of a people:

> To illustrate a certain point, he described what I interpreted to be his own blunder, as he did not in any way reflect upon the eruditions of others. He said that without investigating he had understood that the city of Paducah was named after an Indian chief. After building a monument to the said gentleman, that the baptismal name had been selected for quite a different reason and that there stood a monument to a man who never lived.

This account was reported in the Louisville papers and Paducah's press took umbrage. Taft further exasperated the citizens of Paducah in a letter dated March 17 to the *Paducah Evening Sun* that was reported on page one. He affirmed that the

On March 24, 1916, the Louisville Times *attempted to settle the dispute about the legendary Chief Paduke. The cartoon, which appeared on the front page, looks suspiciously like noted Paducah writer, correspondent, actor, radio and TV host Irvin S. Cobb.*

work was called Paducah in the studio but that it was meant to symbolize the spirit of the city, not to portray a person of uncertain lineage like Paduke. Civic hackles bristled in Paducah. Bradley was portrayed as effeminate, and thus unreliable. Louisville papers continued to tweak the pride of the "Pearl of the Purchase." Other cities joined in, causing Irvin Cobb, Paducah's favorite son and noted journalist, to enter the fray from New York, defending the legend with wit and literary weight. Finally, the Louisville press suggested a solution by showing a drawing of a rather pudgy Indian that could be symbolic of Paducah. In fact, it looked remarkably like Cobb who once worked for that paper while in Louisville.

The real story of the naming of Paducah is more interesting than the legend. Dr. John P. Dyson, formerly from Paducah, published the definitive article on this issue in the *Register of the Kentucky Historical Society* in the spring of 1994:

> In the final analysis, there is no evidence for the claim that William Clark ever had a Chickasaw Indian friend named Paducah or anything else. . . . One must conclude that Clark called the future city PA-DU-CAH solely in order to memorialize and reprove the willful destruction of a once mighty and respected people. . . . For Clark the Padoucas had been deliberately and thoughtlessly annihilated at the instigation of a European greed and depredation to which the United States in its turn had lamentably fallen heir. Moreover, it is likely that he meant through the symbolic christening of his new town to shame national policymakers openly for continuing to abet the ongoing debasement of the tribes west of the Mississippi in his often-unavailing custody.

While the Clark claim was in limbo, settlers did arrive and build rude huts. Robert S. Davis remembered this event in an 1884 interview. Davis came down the Ohio from Harrison County, Kentucky, in 1821. He recounted that the first house at the present site of Paducah was a round-log cabin, about 16 feet square, erected by James and William Pore, brothers, in April 1821 at the foot of what is now Broadway:

> At that time there were only four families in the place, viz: the two Pores, J.D. Martin, and one other whose name is not recalled. Other early names include Charles Ferguson and John Rollins. James Davis, his wife and three sons, Robert S., Isaac, and Jacob, came down the Ohio on a flatboat that originated on a tributary of the Licking River.

After William Clark received clear title to Paducah, he authorized George Woolfolk to act as his agent with instructions to clear out "squatters" or sell them lots.

Robert Fletcher made the original plat of Paducah, as William Clark resided in St. Louis. Clark had the plat recorded June 18, 1830. On January 11, the town had been incorporated with 12 blocks with 12 lots in each block. The frontage of each block was 57.5 feet and the depth was 173 feet, exclusive of a 12-foot alley. Twenty-four small lots were located along the river. Front Street (or Water Street) no longer exists.

The names of the other streets have changed over the years. Initially, streets running perpendicular to the Ohio River were Clark, Washington, Court, Broadway, and Jefferson. The cross streets were Main, Market, Locust, and Oak.

Pore cabin, built c. 1830, is reported to be the one of the first structures in the community.

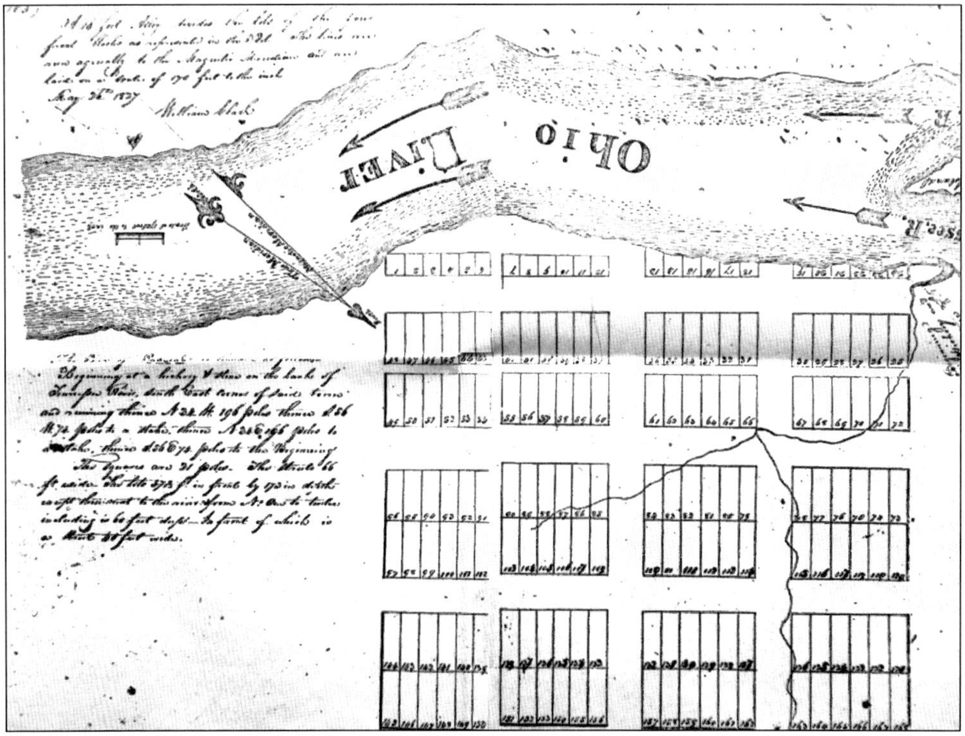

This 1827 plat of Paducah was recorded in 1830. (Courtesy McCracken County records.)

This area became Old Town when the “first addition” (allowed by an amendment enacted by the general assembly in 1833) extended the limits of the town to Ninth Street. Lateral growth followed in 1836 and in 1856. The patterns of enlarging the boundaries since 1856 have retained the river as the focus of the community and have been regular until the 1950s—that is, both perpendicular and lateral extension occurred at the same time. Shifting residential zones began to follow technological innovations that allowed residents to commute greater distances to work while escaping the congestion and pollution that resulted from the arrival of more and more people.

Paducah was the last town to develop in the Purchase region of Kentucky. The opening of the lands west of the Tennessee River after the Chickasaw treaty was further delayed because of a depressed economy, the dispute over the correct boundary between Kentucky and Tennessee, and the dispute over the two claims to the mouth of the Tennessee. The nation also was just recovering from a major depression that began in 1819. The first sale of land west of the Tennessee was held at Princeton in Caldwell County and produced very few takers.

Two towns came into being to meet the needs of prospective settlers: Columbus was designated as the seat of Hickman County, which initially included the entire Purchase region in Kentucky; and Wadesboro became the location of the land office. From these two locations at either end of the region, the pattern of settlement spread out through the region. As soon as sufficient population was present, the original act authorizing settlement provided for the creation of Calloway, Graves, and McCracken Counties. By the time Paducah was laid out, towns and villages throughout the area had more than nine years' head start. Roads linked the region into a functional economic, political, and social entity. That Paducah was able to capture a primary position in the Purchase before 1850 is surprising, considering its late start. At first, Paducah was not even the seat of the county government.

The act authorizing settlement in the Purchase specified that the region should be governed by Hickman County, with its seat at Columbus, until such time as sufficient population was present to warrant further division into Calloway, Graves, and McCracken Counties. Calloway broke away in January 1822, Graves followed in February 1824, and McCracken organized on the third Monday in January 1825. The act authorizing McCracken County provided that the seat of the new county was to be located in township 6; however, no suitable site was found there. An act of the legislature approved December 9, 1825, appointed commissioners to seek out a new location.

This became Wilmington, and the town was completed by January 1827. Two years later, a courthouse rose in the center of the town. For a time it appeared that this hamlet would become the center of the economic and political life of the county; however, flooding made that impossible. By an act approved December 10, 1831, the seat of government moved to the new community of Paducah. When the court of McCracken County was transferred from Wilmington to Paducah, the river was at flood stage. In consequence, Braxton Small, the clerk, carried all the records himself in a small skiff. Small figured prominently in the life of the city and the county. He married Grace Walters on March 1, 1831, in the first recorded marriage in Paducah. His daughter Adelaide was born December 23, 1831, the first child born in the town. At the time, McCracken extended to the Mississippi River; thus, the location at the mouth of the Tennessee was not near the center of the county, but there it stayed. Later, Ballard separated from McCracken, taking off the western part of the county.

The administration of the government of Paducah falls under three separate systems: village, third-class city, and second-class city. Until 1856, a board of trustees controlled Paducah. From 1856 until 1901, a mayor and a board of councilmen directed the city. After a special census conducted in 1901 showed that the city had more than the 20,000 residents necessary to qualify as a second-class city under the new Kentucky Constitution, Paducah changed to a system having four aldermen elected at large from the city in addition to the previous arrangement of a mayor and two representatives from each of the six wards. To effect this change, the state legislature secured an amendment that altered the city charter. Today Paducah enjoys the governance of a mayor, city manager, and commissioners. Unlike the commissioners, the mayor serves a four-year term, and, after 2001, can be re-elected once.

The first election for trustees for Paducah took place on May 2, 1831, at the home of George Dunn. Three days later, the first board convened. F.A. Harrison assumed the chair and called Thomas J. Flournoy, George Dunn, Robert Enders, and Dr. Robert Fletcher to order. The trustees made Ruben Laughlin the city's clerk and assessor while James C. Calhoun became the new collector. Valentine Owen agreed to serve as overseer of the streets. Their first order of business was the removal of some fences that stood across designated streets in the town. The question of the use of the riverfront arose and continued to occupy the city leaders on many future occasions as keelboats, broad horns, flatboats, rafts, and later, steamboats were both a major source of revenue to the town and a continuing menace to the health of the community. It was not uncommon for plagues such as cholera to arrive by river craft, especially in the summer.

After the election of June 15, 1833, James McPherson emerged as the unanimous choice for chairman of the trustees. Others elected along with McPherson included John Hynes, David Smith, Archibald W. Taylor, and John F. Harris. Braxton Small was the clerk (a post he also held in the county government) and Robert Enders became the town treasurer. Gustavus A. Flournoy was appointed assessor and was instructed to compile a list of all white males over 21 and all African-American males over 16 for the purpose of a poll tax. In addition to this routine business, the trustees appointed a board of health. This board began to enforce new sanitary regulations, especially for the riverfront. The instructions to the board empowered them to report any violations of public health to the supervisor of the streets for immediate action. The prime target for this inspection was the condition among the itinerant craft that persisted in ignoring the ban on such craft from the area fronting on Water Street.

Another reason for such a pronouncement was that the town profited from the sale of the use of the space along the riverfront to vendors of wood for fueling passing steamboats. Non-residents were denied the privilege of piling wood for sale on public landings unless they paid the town collector a tax of 12.5¢ per cord. The town also kept a wary eye on the waterfront because of the threat of plague. Cholera arrived in 1832 and repeatedly returned, slowly progressing upstream from New Orleans each year. Smallpox hit John Wilson and Pearce Jones of Paducah on March 16, 1836, but cholera was much more dangerous.

The disease arrived in 1832 on the *Freedom*, which landed with 17 bodies aboard. In 1840, there was a milder outbreak; however, in 1851, ten died. But nothing prepared the community for the outbreak in 1873. The *John Kilgore* stopped at Paducah en route from New Orleans and deposited the plague. Before it was over, 60 deaths occurred. The last victim of the disease was a carpenter, who occupied the last coffin in Paducah.

Dr. Ruben Saunders, the maternal grandfather of Irvin Cobb, noted author of local color, correspondent, and movie star, treated a young African-American female who suffered mortally from the pangs of cholera. Saunders reportedly gave her a massive dose of morphine laced with atropine, a derivative of belladonna, perhaps to ease her suffering and allow her easy passage out of her plight. He was surprised at the result. She fell into a deep coma and on waking days later, her system had healed itself. For a while this treatment was touted as a cure for cholera. Now all that is needed is a needle and the knowledge to inject a saline solution.

In addition to keeping contagious disease in check and fulfilling their basic roles of government administration, cities are expected to provide residents with other services like waste disposal and protection of the environment. Paducahans proved lax in providing proper disposal of their solid waste. The board of health took cognizance of this fact in 1833 by empowering the supervisor of Paducah to "proceed immediately under the superintendence of the board of health to remove, or destroy beyond the corporation or destroy all nuisancez [*sic*] which may be found in the streets." It was not uncommon for butchers to dump the viscera of slain animals "into the streets where roaming hogs like to wallow in the deep mud holes after eating."

A reliable source of potable water was a perennial problem until 1884, when the city granted a private corporation the right to construct a modern system. Piped water was an unknown luxury in 1833 when the trustees first had to deal with the problem of supplying an adequate supply of drinking water. John Hynes and Davis Smith were authorized to let a contract for a public well. The council minutes of July 22 specified the purchase of a pump, but this evidently did not materialize and a bucket served for many years.

The well required constant attention. Frequently, it had to be cleaned. For various reasons the life of a bucket proved to be short and caused the board much grief. Misuse of the bucket led to an ordinance on July 11, 1834, providing for fines for free folk or lashes on "the lower back" for slaves who allowed the bucket to drop too rapidly and become damaged. By June 2, 1835, the trustees had to clean the well and expand its size.

This aerial view shows the merging of the Tennessee and Ohio Rivers and the "chute" (upper right). (JJ.)

This view inside the market house shows the vendors' stalls. (JJ.)

Early in 1833, a special committee was appointed to inspect the chimney of a small house to ascertain if any danger to neighboring structures existed and, if so, the commissioners were to have the chimney made safe. Conditions required a similar committee to reassess the conditions in 1834. Later, the committee reported back to the trustees that extensive renovation would be necessary among the structures on the waterfront lots, particularly those numbered 1 to 12. William W. Lay, chairman of the board, was empowered to let a contract authorizing the purchase of four fire hooks and two ladders.

Vigilance alone was not enough to safeguard property from fires. Nor were fire hooks and ladders sufficient equipment for any growing community. Immediately after the extensive damage from fire suffered by the town in 1838, G. Flournoy, John Wilson, and S.B. Halsed were empowered to purchase a fire engine for the town. Firefighting was to remain a volunteer duty until 1882 and, while willing, these amateurs could not cope with a major conflagration, such as that of 1852. The City did build a two-story brick fire station on what is now Third and Tennessee in 1854 as a direct consequence of the disastrous blaze of 1852, which burned whole blocks and forced Paducah to reconsider its fire protection.

Being on a major transportation route, Paducah early came into contact with traveling players, charlatans, circuses, and other denizens of the world of entertainment. At a meeting of the board held June 3, 1834, it was resolved that "no transit theatrical companies, ventriloquists, or slight [*sic*] of hand performers, or men exhibiting wax figures, or caravans of animals, or any other exhibition or show be permitted to exhibit or perform without paying $5 in advance to the Supervisor." Apparently this fee did not deter shows nor was it intended to prevent performers from entertaining at Paducah. R. Letton paid $12.50 for a permit to perform in Paducah in 1837. The bill of fare available to audiences in the 1830s included F.C. Combs, who was exhibiting human skulls and a specimen of the fine arts as an interesting combination of the lurid and the edifying. An anaconda was to be seen at the Rising Sun Tavern at the same time. In passing, it might be worth noting that it did not take a work of art to attract the attention of the citizens of Paducah. The regular meeting of the council for July 7, 1834, was called off until the next day so that the members of the council could attend the trial of Harvey Reaves for murder. Reaves later was executed.

Stray companies of actors were not the only targets of local taxes. Families were taxed for owning more than one dog after a meeting of the board held June 7, 1834. Also taverns, coffee houses, and other places selling liquor were subject to taxation. Rather than a laissez faire attitude, the town government in this period of Paducah's past reflects an attempt by the elected officials to control thoroughly and absolutely the commerce of the community. This attitude is reflected in the operation of the market.

In early towns, the local market was the core of the community. Originally conceived early in 1836, the Paducah market was constructed by August of that year. It was a frame structure initially, measuring 60 feet in length by 33 feet in width. The cost was $464.50, not counting replacement of the original wooden "pillows" with brick, or the flooring, which came later. The market had a shingle roof and was weather-boarded and painted. Immediately the market was accepted and put to use. Stalls rented on an annual basis, with B.B. Jones leasing the northeast corner stall for $8 per year on August 6, 1838. In Paducah's early stage of development, the central market had monopoly control over the sale and distribution of produce. Farmers from the area brought their wares to sell at the market and citizens became accustomed to going to the market each day for the necessities of the household.

The vitality of Paducah, its organization, and its growth depended upon the town's role as the center of distribution of goods and services to the surrounding hinterland. Located as Paducah was on two major inland waterways, the trade was of prime importance to the development of the town. The fact that Paducah soon became a break-in-bulk point for cargo leaving the Mississippi and Ohio Rivers for the Cumberland (to Nashville and beyond) and the Tennessee (which was navigable as far as Muscle Shoals, Alabama, at that time) helped shape the future of the new community. In 1821, it still took 17 days to travel against the current of the Mississippi and the Ohio from New Orleans to Louisville.

In the journal that Quintus Quincy Quigley kept from 1859 until 1908, this picture of Paducah in 1838 appears: "We reached Paducah about sundown after a weary day's travel. I suffering more than the others but soon forgot about everything else in the sight of the river and other new features and facts of the wild. Paducah at this time was but a small town with perhaps five or six hundred population and mud holes, ravines and marshes all along Broadway to within half a square of the river."

2. Town Growth: 1830–1860

In the period from its inception until the start of the Civil War, Paducah continued to make improvements in its infrastructure, attract new business, and mature its social and political institutions. Attention was given to the grading of streets, construction of sidewalks, paving of some streets in the business district, and improvement of the town's docking facilities. These improvements helped attract new firms and industries such as the Marine Ways. In 1843, Elijah Murray of St. Louis devised a system of eight rails planted perpendicular to the river that allowed both barges and boats to be pulled out of the water by a cradle for refitting and repairs. This facility opened in March 1854. The firm operated until 1924. Today, other firms continue to provide a similar service to the operating equipment of the inland water system of the nation.

In 1842, Watts, Given & Co. established a wharf boat company. As time passed, this facility served not only Paducah, but also smaller communities up the Ohio, Tennessee, and Cumberland Rivers. Roustabouts off-loaded cargo to smaller packets with a draft shallow enough to navigate past the rapids at Eddyville, Kentucky, on the Cumberland and continue on to Nashville and beyond. Other vessels went north on the Ohio and up the Wabash in Indiana, or to the Smallwood plantation on the Tradewater River in Union County, Kentucky. Others funneled goods to farms and communities on the various creeks and bayous off the main channel of the Tennessee River in Tennessee, Mississippi, and Alabama. Hogsheads of tobacco rolled down the main street of Paducah en route to New Orleans and from there to Africa, Europe, and the West Indies.

The day-to-day demands of commerce required additional assets to maintain growth. There was a glaring lack of coin and currency to conduct business. The demand for an adequate means of exchange often required merchants to act as bankers by giving negotiable receipts for goods received. These notes often served as money. Finally, the town set up a municipal bank authorized to issue currency. This agency, known as The Exchange Bank of Paducah, began operation in 1837. The bank issued bills in five denominations ranging in value from 6.25¢ to 75¢ for a total of $500. These bills were redeemable at a ratio of one for five in the following currencies: $100 in Kentucky bills, $200 in Alabama currency, and $200 in bills from Tennessee. The treasurer of the new bank was Braxton Small, who served as county clerk and as a trustee of Paducah at various times.

This map shows the patterns of expansion of the town of Paducah. (Courtesy Office of Planning, City of Paducah.)

Prior to changing its status from that of a town to a third-class city, Paducah acquired two other banks. In 1845, a branch of the Bank of Louisville opened at Paducah with a capital stock of $200,000. James Campbell served as the first president and Adam Rankin was the cashier. In 1852, the Commerce Bank of Kentucky took a building at the corner of Third and Broadway. L.M. Flournoy was president and James M. Dallam was cashier. Initial capitalization was listed at $2 million. In addition to these banks, William F. Norton and Watts, Given & Co. began making loans in 1850. While not formal banks, they served many of the same functions for the community. Watts, Given & Co. failed in the recession following the Civil War along with the Commerce Bank.

The census of 1850 listed 1,141 males and 972 females in Paducah. This included 374 slaves and 18 free African Americans. A wide variety of firms and services were available to the citizens at that time; one could buy agricultural implements and ambrotypes. There were 21 attorneys available (and probably needed) to settle land disputes, protect property, and uphold the law in a raw river town. Nine carpenters and two carriage makers assured those wishing for more room or a better buggy got prompt attention. Three bakers matched three bankers. Also, customers could employ three "good" tailors, three suppliers of shoes, three sellers of jewelry, and one silversmith, John Beauchamp. For a new town, the variety of stores and services is surprising. Fair's cornet band was available for festive occasions, as were a brewery, 21 coffee houses, a distillery, and 4 hotels. Louis Mueller's Pleasure Garden also promised potables. The more conservative could point with pride to four schools, two seminaries, and a seller of magazines.

The day March 10, 1856, marked a pivotal point in the progress of Paducah, as the community became a third-class city. The following August, J.H. Gardner was elected mayor. By 1860, the population exceeded 6,000.

While steamboats dominated commerce and passenger service until after the Civil War, Paducah early on determined to seek a new mode of transport—the railroads. This new fad began to gather momentum by the mid-1850s, when Congress made grants of public land to encourage the completion of a railroad running from the Great Lakes to the Gulf of Mexico. Thus, the Illinois Central Railroad came into being to link Chicago with the Ohio River. Another line (the Mobile & Ohio) ran from the Gulf of Mexico to the Ohio; however, since no suitable point was found on the Ohio, the line extended to Columbus, Kentucky, on the Mississippi River. Cars, cargo, and passengers were transferred by steamboat from there to Cairo, Illinois, and on to Chicago by rail. Paducah was determined not to be left out of the new era.

The General Assembly of Kentucky helped Paducah fulfill its railroad dreams in a session of the legislature in 1851–1852 that allowed cities to issue bonds to help in the construction of railroads. The minutes of the trustees on March 1, 1852, reported that the town agreed to buy stock in the proposed New Orleans & Ohio Railroad. This line was to run 60 miles south from Paducah to join with lines running from the Ohio to either New Orleans or Mobile. The estimated cost was $1 million and Paducah agreed to contribute $200,000. Judge L.M. Flournoy, Judge James Campbell, John W. Crockett, S.F. Singleton, B.F. Givens, Henry Enders, James Langstaff, and William Norton were among the promoters.

A woodyard at the confluence of the Tennessee and Ohio Rivers at Paducah was a source of profit to the city. (Courtesy SB.)

This view of the market house was captured in the 1880s. (Courtesy McCPL.)

The engineer selected to supervise the construction of the railroad was Lloyd Tilghman, a member of a distinguished family from Maryland and a graduate of West Point who had considerable experience on various lines in North and Central America.

Work on grading began in 1853. By July 4, 1854, the road reached Florence, a distance of 7 miles south of Paducah. Independence Day festivities included an excursion and a barbecue. In *Main Line of Mid-America,* Carlton J. Corliss wrote, "People drove in carriages and ox-teams and came on foot and horse and on mule-back from miles to witness for the first time in their lives the thrilling spectacle of a roaring 'iron horse' consuming wood and water and belching forth smoke, fire, and steam as it pulled a train of cars at the amazing speed of 15 miles per hour." Corliss noted that the primitive engine was "about as big as a thresher" and pulled two small flat cars. Passengers feared they would not be able to breath at such a rapid rate. The engine was called the *James Campbell* after the president of the line. At the controls was John Lawson, engineer.

In his later years Lawson claimed to have been the engineer on the first successful railroad in his native England in 1827. Lawson said he worked for George Stephenson on the Manchester to Liverpool railroad. His claim is contrary to most generally accepted histories of railroads that give the honor of operating the first successful railroad trip to George Stephenson. Lawson said he worked for Stephenson and actually was at the controls of the machine on the trip. Lawson came to the United States with an engine manufactured by Stephenson, which was called the *Herald* after the vessel that brought him and the engine from England. Lawson claimed to have been at the throttle when the *Herald* first ran in the United States on the 10-mile run from Baltimore to Green Springs in 1829.

Leaving the employment of Stephenson, Lawson worked for the Baldwin Locomotive Works in Philadelphia before migrating to the Ohio Valley and Paducah in 1840. At Paducah, he became active with river engines and owned and operated a small number of packets. During the Civil War, Lawson threw his lot with the Confederacy, supervising the construction of a steam ram while at Yazoo, Mississippi. After the fall of Vicksburg, Lawson left the river, took up a musket, and served as an aged private in the 3rd Kentucky Cavalry until the end of the war. He remained active until his death and for a time worked in Paducah tending the boiler of the federal building constructed there during the administration of Democratic President Grover Cleveland. Finally, Lawson moved to St. Louis, where he died in 1901.

The New Orleans & Ohio was completed in 1860 to Troy, Tennessee, where it linked with lines going either to New Orleans or to Mobile. At the same time, the link also meant that for the first time, Paducah was in direct communication with the cities on the Gulf of Mexico and also with those on the Atlantic Ocean by the use of the telegraph and relays. The end of isolation also meant that events far removed from Paducah affected the growing community. In the decade from 1850 to 1860, new advances in technology seemed to rush into use with increasing rapidity.

News reached Paducah by telegraph and the local newspapers blared forth with ever more strident voices at each crisis. R.R. Willis published *The Express*

Once built, railroads required constant maintenance to operate. Until about 1950, this involved hard manual labor and constant watchfulness by the section crews, such as this one supervised by Lee Robertson with the able assistance of Clarence L., his son, who had the responsibility to keep the water bucket and the vital pocket watch.

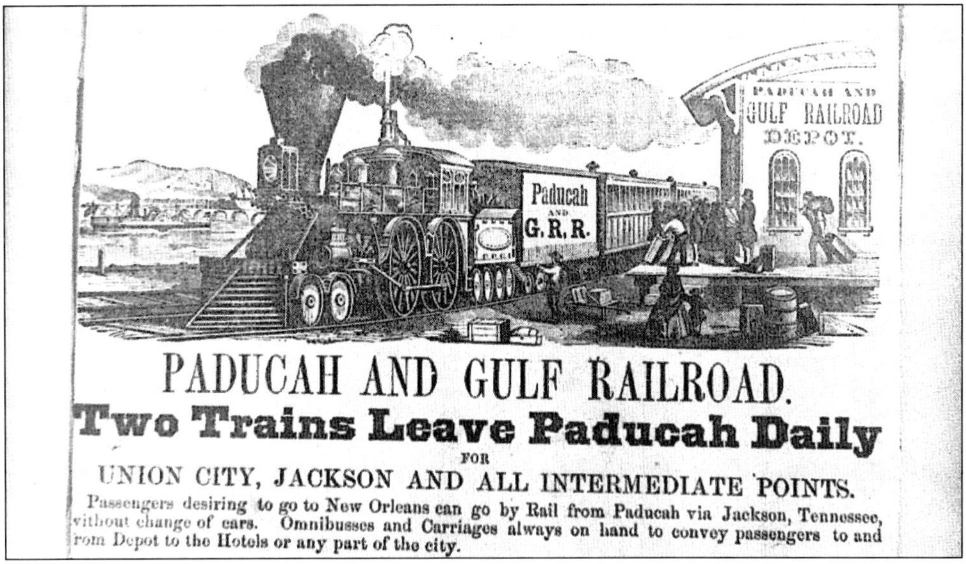

This 4-4-0 engine was typical of the earliest locomotives on the original New Orleans & Ohio and the later Paducah & Gulf Railroad.

from about 1834 to 1835. This paper followed the Whig sentiments espoused by Henry Clay, by Lexington politicians, and by most other Kentuckians of the time. With the exception of Paducah, Kentucky's share of the Jackson Purchase became identified with Andrew Jackson's party, the Democrats. Paducah could not always overcome the rural Democrats and as a result, McCracken County usually joined the rest of the Purchase in supporting the Democratic Party.

Paducah and McCracken County were anomalies in the voting patterns in the Purchase. Neither existed in the presidential election of 1824, when Calloway, Hickman, and Graves Counties voted overwhelmingly for Andrew Jackson in a losing effort. In 1828, slightly more than 80 percent of the voters in the Purchase sided with Old Hickory as Jackson won the White House. This margin dropped slightly in 1832, when 79.8 percent of the voters throughout the Purchase again supported the Democratic ticket.

Beginning in 1836, a different pattern developed. McCracken County was the lone supporter of William Henry Harrison and the new Whig party in the Purchase. Of the 255 votes cast, 106, or 41.6 percent, went to Martin Van Buren, the Democrat, while 149, or 58.4 percent, favored Harrison. In 1844, McCracken voted Whig, losing slightly in the total percentage of votes cast (56.8 percent). In fact, the total vote was down from 652 in 1840 to only 451 in 1844. Henry Clay received 256 votes to 195 against the successful Democrat James K. Polk. The Whigs kept their majority of McCracken votes in 1848. Of the 715 votes cast, the Whigs got 407, or 56.9 percent, thus helping put native Kentuckian Zachary Taylor into the White House even if only for a short time. (He died on July 9, 1850, and was succeeded by Millard Fillmore, who favored Clay's and Boyd's compromise legislation.)

Congressman Linn Boyd played a major role in the Compromise of 1850, along with Senator Henry Clay of Kentucky. Boyd moved to Paducah, won election as lieutenant governor of Kentucky, but died before taking office. Boyd served two terms as Speaker of the U.S. House of Representatives.

Quigley wrote of Boyd in his journal on December 24, 1859, "since my last the Hon. Linn Boyd before spoken of in this memoranda has gone to his home in the unknown future. He was in many respects a noble man. He was fresh in his views as a public man with a record almost invulnerable. As a private citizen he was bland and agreeable rather selfish and of last years retiring. Let the evil be forgotten and the good remembered."

In Paducah, Q.Q. Quigley supported the Whig party until it began to disintegrate after the turmoil culminating in the Compromise of 1850 regarding slavery in the federal territories. Senator Henry Clay, a Whig, teamed with Congressman Linn Boyd, a Democrat and fellow Kentuckian, to get the compromise through Congress. Boyd represented the First Congressional District of Kentucky seven times. In recognition of his contribution to the compromise, Boyd twice won election as Speaker of the House of Representatives from 1851 to 1855. Later, he moved to Paducah and won election as the lieutenant governor of Kentucky on the Democratic ticket in 1859. Boyd went to Philadelphia for treatment for a disease of the urinary organs, which failed. He died before he could take office.

The election of 1852 saw McCracken voting Democratic; however, the vote cast was light. Franklin Pierce might have carried both McCracken and Paducah, but with little enthusiasm. The following election, McCracken returned to its role as a maverick by supporting the American, or Know-Nothing ticket rather than the victorious James Buchanan, giving 660 of 1,165 votes to Fillmore. In 1860, the bulk of the voters in McCracken voted for the moderate John Bell (710). Stephen Douglas, the northern Democrat, got 280 while the sitting vice president, John C. Breckinridge of Kentucky, received 244 votes for the extreme southern wing of the Democratic party. The victorious Abraham Lincoln of the new Republican party received a total of eight votes.

3. Kentucky Tries Neutrality

Like a craft without the ability to steer caught in uncertain eddies and undertows, the United States of America seemed destined to end in a deadly drift toward disunion as 1860 came to a close. In this period of great uncertainty, Q.Q. Quigley wrote the following thoughts on page 100 of his journal on Friday night, December 21, 1860:

> For several months the dread of dissolution of our union has awakened the deepest concern in the minds of our people. The dread preceding principally from the belief that South Carolina would go out under the doctrine (erroneously, I think) that each state has a right under the constitution to secede. She, being the proof of the sufficiency of the cause. In the exercise of that assumed principle she, South Carolina, on the 19th has conventioned, called by the legislature, passed a resolution declaring her disserverance from the Union. This I regard as the apple of discord, as a new Pandora's box opened up scattering over the whole country seeds which shall ripen with revolt, revolution, Civil War, and a thousand untold and incalculable evils that time alone can fully develop. The principle once established that a state can thus with impunity throw off her allegiance to the general government only establishes the fact that in reality we never had such and that our boasted constitution was simply a sublime farce and the changes in making may but foreshadow by her change from sunshine to storm the political state we are reaching.

Citizens of Paducah met in Gardner's Hall on December 22 to discuss national events. According to the journal entry of Quigley on December 24, many attended with the hope of taking some action to preserve the union, if possible, and give their weight to one side or the other. The atmosphere seethed with hostile undercurrents:

> I at once discovered antagonistic elements were assembled and from remarks dropped by a few men soon learned that it was generally undisclosed what resolutions were and who were to offer them and that sides had been taken in advance and that there was no sense of grave and serious deliberation pervading the meeting but that there were a few

> men self-constituted the champions of the occasion for the purpose of manufacturing for themselves prestige and popularity.

R.B.J. Twyman offered a resolution Quigley belittled. He then wrote of Judge James Campbell's taking the floor:

> Although I had been apprised that he was fast going over to dissolution I was not prepared for the ultra-Southern ground and defiance breathed by the resolution. They were well written and in fine, strong and dignified language but full of resistance. He then followed in his speech supporting them and as he progressed becoming more and more inflammatory until he equaled a rabid excitement.

Quigley remembered that only a few short weeks prior Campbell was "the most earnest Union sounding speaker in the canvas for President." J.J.A. King took the floor with what Quigley considered "a mere recapitulation of the glory of our institutions." It seemed that the debate now rested with Campbell and King. Quigley tried to offer a compromise but was denied. He left only to learn later that King's motion carried after considerable squabble and confusion. As the contending sides matured their views, the differences became more pronounced and feelings expressed in harsher terms. Quigley reflected this growing schism in his closing entry. "What will be the end? None can certainly predict."

When Quigley went to his office on Christmas Day, an ominous sight greeted him that he felt was a prelude to violence and boded ill for the well being of the community:

> The first thing that arrested my attention in coming to my office was an effigy hung by the neck to the telegraph wire at the corner of Broadway and Locust Street with a large card attached inscribed "The fate of a disunionist." The figure also had a copy of the *Paducah Herald* in its hand and the effigy was said to represent J.C. Noble, its editor. After a short time the mayor had it taken down and then the boys put it on a dray and hauled it up and down the streets and finally in front of Noble's office on Main and then burned it.

The election of Abraham Lincoln in November 1860 had been the signal for the South to secede as the year waned. A convention met in Charleston, South Carolina, on December 20 and passed an ordinance to the effect that "the union now subsisting between South Carolina and the other States, under the name of the 'United States of America,' is hereby dissolved." Other states followed: Mississippi, January 9, 1861; Florida, January 10; Alabama, January 11; Georgia, January 19; Louisiana, January 26; and Texas, after putting the question to the voters, February 1. In these troubled times, border states did not rush to make a decision. Kentucky, in particular, hesitated, as did the people in Paducah.

R.B.J. Twyman was an avowed Democrat, yet the Paducah editor noted "when the telegraph announced that South Carolina had seceded from the Union, there were not half a dozen out-spoken secessionists in Paducah, but as State after State went out and took their stand by the side of South Carolina, the secession element gained strength, and one by one, the people turned over to the side of the Southern Confederacy." Twyman continued, "The Union party, however, maintained the ascendancy in Paducah until military forces of South Carolina fired upon Fort Sumter on April 14, 1861. As soon as the wires flashed the news of the surrender of this fortification throughout the country, the war was considered as having commenced, and all were wild with excitement. Men and women seemed really to go mad." Firing began at 4:30 a.m. eastern time. In Paducah, the telegraph brought the news while the town slept. When they heard about the opening shots, Paducahans lit lanterns and hung them on their gates as a gesture of support. By first light, the town glowed.

Beriah Magoffin, the governor, and Simon Bolivar Buckner, head of the state guard, were sympathetic to the Southern cause; however, they could not sway the majority of the general assembly that Kentucky should secede. After hostilities began at Fort Sumter, Magoffin rebuffed the request of the secretary of war to furnish troops to put down the rebellion. A similar denial was given the new Confederate States of America, but in softer terms. In this impasse, Magoffin finally announced that Kentucky would stand aloof from the conflict and fight either side that violated its soil. Presidents Lincoln and Davis both felt that it was imperative to have Kentucky and were willing to wait, each hoping that events would turn the state toward their side. In the meantime, the state guard was alerted. The commander of the guard in Western Kentucky was Lloyd Tilghman of Paducah, a graduate of West Point.

One must remember that no bridges existed over the Ohio River in 1860 and that Kentucky trade, tradition, and family ties were linked southward. Southern sentiment led to a secession convention held in Mayfield, seat of Graves County and next door to McCracken County, to determine if the Purchase region needed to secede from Kentucky and join the Confederacy. The movement failed; however, Henry Burdett, congressman from the First District of Kentucky, was the only member of the U.S. House to be ejected for supporting secession.

Confederate Gideon J. Pillow, commanding at Memphis, and John C. Frémont, commanding Federal forces from St. Louis, both watched the neutrality of Kentucky closely. The prize was the high ground at Columbus, which promised a point from which traffic on the Mississippi River could be interdicted. Also, Paducah, at the mouth of the Tennessee on the Ohio and the terminus of the New Orleans & Ohio Railroad, was vital to both sides.

Reports came to the attention of Pillow that Federal troops threatened Columbus. The mayor of that town wrote Pillow and begged him to get there first. Buckner, head of the state guard, also heard reports that a Federal patrol boat saw a rebel flag flying at Columbus. The *City of Alton* approached the town with guns run out. The flag was there, but, rather than violate the neutrality of

Lloyd Tilghman is dressed in a Kentucky State Guard uniform.

Kentucky, a party from the boat consisting of the pilot and another civilian jumped ashore, ripped down the flag as a trophy, jumped back on the moving craft, and returned to their base at Cairo, Illinois. An account in the *Louisville Daily Courier*, June 1, 1861, with a Cairo dateline identified William Banks, captain of the boat, and its pilot as the landing party. General George McClellan, commanding officer at Cincinnati, called Buckner and Magoffin to enforce the neutrality of Kentucky. Lloyd Tilghman's command was called into active service and sent to Columbus to prevent either side from breaking the neutrality.

Tilghman left state service shortly after this incident, and his family left Paducah as well. He went to Guthrie, Tennessee, and formed the 3rd Kentucky about July 29. Before leaving Kentucky, Tilghman turned the state guard over to Ben Hardin Helm, a brother-in-law of President Lincoln who soon followed Tilghman south.

On August 20, 1861, a series of events at Paducah led directly to the entry of Kentucky into the war as an active participant. The United States gunboat *Lexington* "fastened on to the [*W.B.*] *Terry*, cut her cables, and went off down the river" according to Quigley's journal. The action took place at "half past six a.m." and the affair "was handsomely and speedily done" according to Quigley. A Union incursion into Blandville, Kentucky, also was reported. Sadly, Quigley made few other notes during the war, perhaps fearing that his views would offend the occupying authorities.

R.N. Stembel, commander of the Union gunboat, reported the action to Colonel R.J. Oglesby at Cairo as justified. The *W.B. Terry* had been boarded, searched, and seized by Stembel: "I had indisputable proof which examination of her papers found on board confirmed, that she was running in the employment of the Confederacy." Word of Stembel's action reached the area commander, Frémont, who, in turn, sent his own report to General Lorenzo Thomas, adjutant general of the army. "Events had thus transpired clearly indicating the complicity of citizens of Kentucky with the rebel forces, and showing the impracticability of carrying on operation in that direction without involving Kentucky," Frémont wrote.

Three citizens of Paducah and one from Mississippi jointly owned the packet boat *W.B. Terry*. In retaliation for Stembel's action, Captain Johnson, late skipper of the vessel, A.M. Winston, White Fowler, and other Paducah citizens seized the boat *Samuel Orr*, the regular mail packet between Paducah and Evansville, Indiana. This vessel was sent hurriedly up the Tennessee River to the safety of Confederate territory.

Lieutenant General Leonidas Polk, newly in command at Memphis, heard of two events—the appearance of Federal troops across the river from Columbus at Belmont and the seizure of the *W.B. Terry*. Feeling that he could wait no longer for Kentucky to make up its mind, Polk sent a telegram to Governor Magoffin of Kentucky indicating that it was his intention to occupy Columbus before it fell into Federal hands. "I think it is the greatest consequence to the Southern cause in Kentucky or elsewhere that I should be ahead of the enemy in occupying Columbus and Paducah," he wrote. Accordingly, on September 3, 1861, General Pillow led the vanguard of the Confederate army into Hickman while General

The "iron banks" at Columbus, Kentucky, were prized by both North and South. To prevent this site from falling to the Union, General Polk took it upon himself to violate the neutrality of Kentucky in 1861. Grant then seized Paducah.

Polk took personal command of the column numbering between 1,500 and 2,000 men that entered Columbus to the welcoming hurrahs and joyful tears of the partisan population.

J.G. Deupree described the Confederate advance:

> Early in September, the cavalry were ferried across the river and rode to Hickman, Kentucky, whether General [Frank] Cheatham and a brigade of infantry had gone on a steamboat. Dense columns of smoke were visible far up the river. Women and children were screaming in the streets, as we arrived; bugles were sounded; and guns were placed in commanding positions to resist an expected attack, for a large force was believed to be coming down, threatening the capture of Hickman. Union boats were scouting to see what was happening; nevertheless, the population welcomed the rebels as saviors. Pillow's field artillery turned back the wooden scout boats without loss of life on either side.

Ulysses S. Grant now commanded the Federal forces at Cairo. The day after he took command from Richard Oglesby, word came to Grant from a scout who reported that Polk had moved into Kentucky. Grant sent word to Frémont via a messenger that unless he received orders to the contrary, Grant would occupy Paducah. Then, Grant embarked the 9th and 12th Illinois and a four-gun battery of artillery on transports, departed Cairo, and waited in midstream of the Ohio for dawn on the sixth.

Confederate flags were flying in Paducah in anticipation of the imminent arrival of Southern troops, who were expected about noon, according to common report. The unexpected appearance of blue uniforms in this town offended many whose sympathies were ardently Southern. The later Union assumption that all Paducahans were pro-rebel was not conducive to improving relations between the invading force and the townsfolk. However, the presence of so many "plump, small-boned women" more than made up to the troops for the jeers and defiant cries they heard, and they "fell in love with Paducah on sight," as one wrote.

Grant wrote, "When the National troops entered the town the citizens were taken by surprise. I never after saw such consternation depicted on the faces of the people." This surprise was reflected on sleepy faces. "Men, women, and children came out of their doors looking pale and frightened at the presence of the invader. They were expecting rebel troops that day." According to Grant, the rebels had nearly 4,000 men from Columbus and "were at that time within ten or fifteen miles of Paducah on their way to occupy the place." Actually, Frank Cheatham did have a small group near Mayfield and was proceeding toward Paducah when he heard of Grant's move. Once ashore, Grant moved swiftly. He had to. As he recalled, "I had but two regiments and one battery with me; but the enemy did not know this and returned to Columbus. I stationed my troops at best points to guard the roads leading into the city, left the gunboats to guard the river front and by noon was ready to start on my return to Cairo."

Grant tried to assuage the populace. "Before leaving, however, I addressed a short printed proclamation to the citizens of Paducah assuring them of our approaches to the city." He also seized a quantity of supplies including 2 tons of leather destined for the South and other contraband items. Grant left explicit orders for the deportment of the troops to prevent their plundering the populace or aggravating them further than was absolutely necessary. Brigadier Eleazar A. Paine of Illinois was placed in temporary command. Paine and Paducah were destined to share stormy days later in the war when the political general was no longer restrained in his dealings with those known to favor the rebellion.

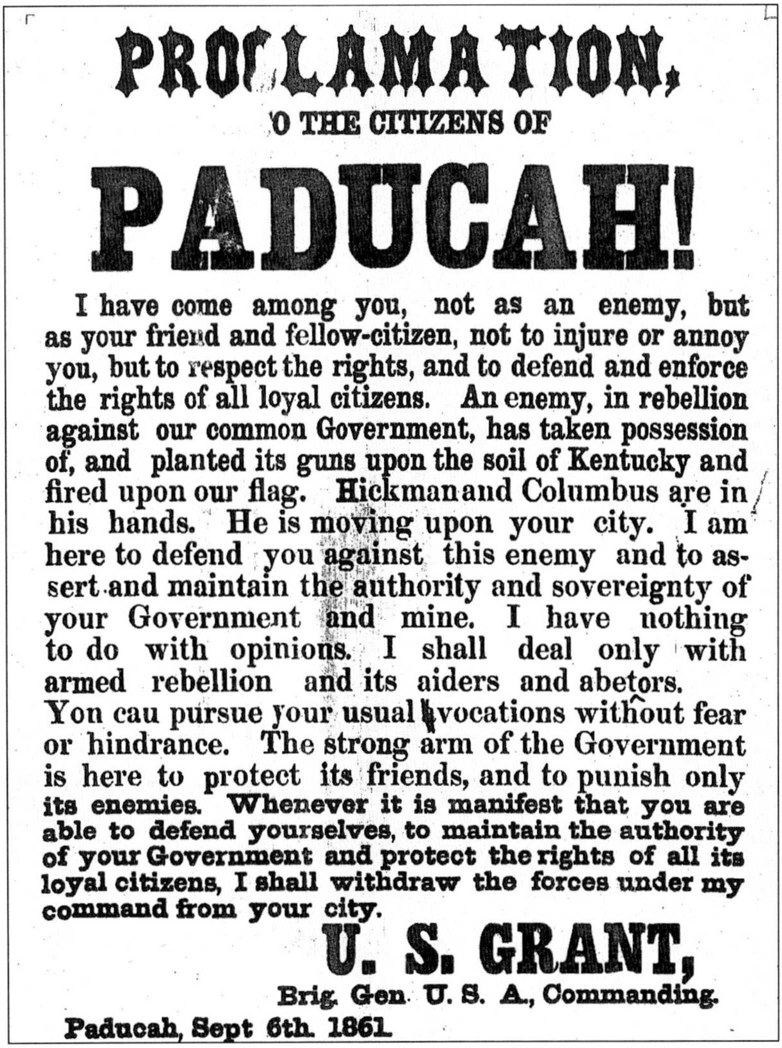

PROCLAMATION,

TO THE CITIZENS OF

PADUCAH!

I have come among you, not as an enemy, but as your friend and fellow-citizen, not to injure or annoy you, but to respect the rights, and to defend and enforce the rights of all loyal citizens. An enemy, in rebellion against our common Government, has taken possession of, and planted its guns upon the soil of Kentucky and fired upon our flag. Hickman and Columbus are in his hands. He is moving upon your city. I am here to defend you against this enemy and to assert and maintain the authority and sovereignty of your Government and mine. I have nothing to do with opinions. I shall deal only with armed rebellion and its aiders and abetors. Yon cau pursue your usual vocations without fear or hindrance. The strong arm of the Government is here to protect its friends, and to punish only its enemies. Whenever it is manifest that you are able to defend yourselves, to maintain the authority of your Government and protect the rights of all its loyal citizens, I shall withdraw the forces under my command from your city.

U. S. GRANT,

Brig. Gen. U. S. A., Commanding.

Paducah, Sept 6th. 1861

Grant issued this hurriedly put-together proclamation (notice the various fonts used) to comfort the citizens of Paducah, many of whom were eagerly awaiting the arrival of rebel troops, including many boys from Paducah. Mayor Tom Wilson re-issued this proclamation for the centennial of Paducah.

4. On the Home Front

Early in 1861, the attitude of the South toward free trade changed. At issue was the trade in cotton that went to the North through the border states, such as Kentucky. The financial panic of 1857 to 1858 had little impact on the South. To many, this meant that if the Northern economy could be disrupted by a denial of Southern raw materials such as cotton, then the ability of the North to wage war would be compromised.

The South began to use cotton as a means of conducting economic warfare and assisting in ongoing diplomatic maneuvering with European nations, hoping to gain recognition. The fact that several neutral border states would suffer as a result of restricting trade in cotton was of secondary importance to the Confederacy at the moment. In the Southern view, the injury that would accrue to the North more than compensated for the ill will generated in the border states. On May 21, the Confederate Congress passed a law that embargoed any shipment of cotton and cotton yards from Confederate states except through Southern ports. (One exception was the provision for shipment across the Rio Grande into Mexico.) Any steamboat or railroad car found carrying cotton products out of the Confederacy in violation of this law was subject to seizure and confiscation for the use of the government.

Kentucky reacted immediately:

> Resolved, by the General Assembly of the Commonwealth of Kentucky, That Kentucky, having as much right to the Mississippi River, and to its free unobstructed navigation as Louisiana or any other State and that right being of vital importance to her people, feels it her duty to herself and to her sister States, at the earliest day, to make this her most solemn protest against any assumption of such power to control the navigation of that river as utterly without right or proper authority, and as what she cannot and will not submit to.

Despite the protest of Kentucky, the Confederacy persisted in its attempt to prevent the Union gaining access to Southern produce. On May 21, other items were added to the embargo. Tobacco, sugar, rice, molasses, syrup, and naval stores were enumerated. This law became effective August 10. In addition to the Confederate government's policy of restriction, Governor Isham Green Harris of

Paducah's riverfront commerce was greatly affected by the Civil War, as seen in this 1861 Leslie's Illustrated *image. This makeshift vessel was fitted with wood and plate iron armor.*

Tennessee also put an embargo on a list of articles. The rebels had, at the time, an additional purpose in these acts. They hoped to illustrate forcibly to Kentucky that the state should be aligned with the South.

After the occupation of Hickman and Columbus by Polk, that officer forbade any trade until his agents bought up all the food and provisions the army needed. He felt this action was warranted to prevent speculators from raising prices. Merchants from Memphis protested this decision to Confederate President Jefferson Davis, who ordered the embargo lifted at once, saying that his government would rather pay higher prices than obstruct free trade. Judah P. Benjamin affirmed this policy: "We have left commerce free in everything but the arms and munitions of war indispensable for defense."

After Pillow and Polk ended the tacit agreement not to enter Kentucky, the Confederate government agreed that any act of their Congress that restricted trade should not apply to those parts of Kentucky that were under the control of Confederate arms. A licensing system came into usage for the benefit of those Kentuckians loyal to the rebel cause, allowing trade in Southern products with the exception of cotton and naval stores. No trade was allowed north of Confederate lines.

The Federal position on trade was evidenced early. The *Cincinnati Daily Gazette* for June 12, 1861, reported that the Federal revenue officers at that city forbade any boat to carry pork, flour, wheat, hay, corn, oats, livestock, arms, or ammunition from there to Paducah and Smithland. The explanation for this embargo was that this section of Kentucky was strongly secessionist in sympathy. Of course, Kentucky was still neutral at this time. People in this area suffered to the point of genuine distress as a result of these regulations. The same issue of this newspaper

After rebel forces took Columbus and Hickman, Brigadier General U.S. Grant seized and occupied Paducah, enforcing severe trade restrictions to keep merchants and others from aiding the South.

notes that several business houses in Paducah were closed, and in distress, and again that a report of this general region said, "There are no groceries, no goods nor money in our section of the State." After the Confederates occupied the western part of the state around Columbus, U.S. Secretary of Treasury Salmon P. Chase declared that the region of Kentucky west of the Cumberland River was in "rebel hands," and that no trade whatever was to be allowed. Again, Paducah was affected without overt cause.

The occupation of Paducah by Grant did little to remove the restrictions placed on trade. Steamers still could not stop between Evansville, Indiana, and Paducah. Ostensibly, loyal men were allowed to engage in trade, but the difficulty was in convincing the Federal agents that one was loyal. Yet, despite all the rules and regulations, trade did exist and most of it was still covert exchange with the Confederacy. One route taken to avoid Federal regulations for a time was across the southern part of Illinois (where the people were sympathetic to the South) through Jonesborough and then across the Mississippi River into Missouri and on southward. While quite circuitous, this route was effective. To break up this trade, Grant ordered all interchange of goods between Kentucky and Illinois halted. Dealers in this illicit traffic were not easily stopped: barrels and boxes containing contraband were marked with seemingly innocent contents. Grant said of one shipment, "Eighty barrels of this freight were whiskey, a character of commerce I would have no objection to being carried on with the South, but there is a probability that some barrels marked whiskey might contain something more objectionable."

No one of Confederate sympathy was permitted to engage in trade, and to safeguard the rights of trade, agents of the Federal government were required to administer the following oath: "I do solemnly swear that I have not by word or action given the slightest aid and comfort to the present rebellion, and that by my conservation and action I will do all I can to discourage and discountenance and overthrow the rebellion, and will use all my influence to restore the authority of the Government of the United States over the States now in rebellion."

As long as the Federal position in Kentucky was one of defense, the attitude toward trade was to prevent any and all intercourse with the South. Treasury agents had to enforce the regulations. At first, they had little difficulty with Northern traders seeking to exploit trade into the South. Once the forces of the Union began to move south, the problem of allowing an expansion of trade became an ever-present burden to most of the commanding officers in the field as well as to treasury agents. Cupidity is a powerful force to quell. Fortunes could be made in contraband cotton. After the fall of Forts Henry and Donelson and the opening of the Mississippi after the evacuation of Columbus and Island Number Ten, a considerable expanse of enemy territory was ripe for plucking.

Early in March 1862, Edwin Stanton, secretary of war, informed General Henry W. Halleck that the act of Congress of July 12, 1861, which prohibited trade with states south of Kentucky and Missouri, remained in force. Instruction by the secretary of the treasury regulated trade with the conquered regions. On March 3, the licensing system and permit system in force on the Ohio and Upper Mississippi also was applied to both the Tennessee and the Cumberland Rivers as well. All baggage and packages taken into this region had to display an official seal. All vehicles, railroad cars, and watercraft were forbidden to carry any merchandise not covered by permits issued by the customhouses. These permits were "not upon trade, or to impede or in any manner interfere with the freedom of legitimate and proper transportation or travel." The surveyors of customs granted these permits. Federal officials were instructed to "use liberally, though cautiously, the discretion with which they are intrusted [*sic*]." Perhaps the customs agents were optimistic, or pressure to obtain these permits was excessive, for on March 28, an order was issued canceling all previous licenses effective April 15. New regulations made it much more difficult to obtain a license. Each boat that traded south of St. Louis or Louisville was required to show their manifest at every port and also had to carry Federal agents called "aids to the revenue," which prevented or supervised taking on any additional cargo along the way.

Soon a Kentuckian had to establish his loyalty before being allowed to engage in local trade. General Jeremiah Tilford Boyle issued an order on October 24, 1862, prohibiting anyone who was disloyal to the Union from shipping produce or goods of any kind in, into, or through the state. These permits cost 20¢ each and those allowing a person residing outside Kentucky to engage in trade with anyone living within the state read as follows: "This is to certify that ___ of ___ County, State of ___ has permission to ship ___ out of and into the State of Kentucky." Kentucky's new governor, Thomas E. Bramlette, bitterly denounced the use of these permits by Federal authorities in the state in a letter to President Lincoln. Bramlette claimed that "the ordinary and necessary trade of the State is now, by military regulations, subjected to restrictions which harass the citizens without any compensating public good and which wears more the phase of subjecting the citizens to odious political tests than looking to public good." It would seem that the Federal bureaucracy rejected the official posture of Kentucky as a loyal state and set out to make each citizen prove his allegiance. Kentuckians continued throughout the war to protest this discriminatory treatment.

While Grant pushed the rebels down the Mississippi, he prohibited "all trading and trafficking or landing of boats" south of Memphis, except at military posts. Trade did not diminish, it flourished. Under the guise of taking on wood, steamers continued to supply rebels with contraband and receive cotton (that was equally contraband, from the Southern point of view). The Federal commander at Memphis charged that the bayous and creeks were teeming with trading steamers that "invite rebel officers and soldiers on board and drink and hobnob together."

A significant date in the commerce of the entire Mississippi Valley was July 8, 1863, when Port Hudson fell four days after the surrender of Vicksburg. The Mississippi once again was open for traffic. President Lincoln rejoiced that the "Father of Waters rolled unvexed to the sea." In Kentucky, opening of the Mississippi River did not end control of trade by agents of the treasury. They continued to discourage and discomfort commercial affairs, particularly by those suspected of rebel sympathies.

The opening of the Mississippi did not immediately restore trade. Congress passed an act on July 2, 1864, granting trade permits to loyal people:

> No goods, wares, or merchandise shall be taken into a State declared in insurrection, or transported therein, except to and from such places and to such monthly amounts as shall have been previously agreed upon in writing by the commanding general of the department in which such places were situated, and an officer designated by the Secretary of the Treasury for that Purpose.

On the military side, the opening of the Mississippi meant that the Confederacy was split in half. Now the Union forces could begin to squeeze the eastern segment to death. This strategy originally had been suggested by Winfield Scott and was called the "Anaconda Plan." Coupled with a naval blockade of rebel ports along the eastern Atlantic shore, the plan worked.

On April 29, 1865, all restrictions on trade east of the Mississippi were removed (except contraband of war), and on June 24, this order was extended to include the region west of the Mississippi. Not until August 29 did the last restriction on trade end and the country was again one economic unit along the inland waterways.

5. The Fatal Thrust

Occupation of Paducah by Union forces led to friction between the troops and the populace that gradually deepened into hatred as time passed. Paducahans did not hesitate to show their displeasure at the presence of the Federals. City officials consulted with the military concerning the elections held in the summer of 1862. This was to comply with the order of General Jeremiah T. Boyle, who became the commander of the Department of Kentucky in June. Boyle issued orders requiring only loyal citizens to run for office. In effect, this order effectively denied members of the Democratic Party from participating in the election.

Officers moved into private houses and businesses, such as the bakery of George Oehlschlaeger and the gun shop of Ferd Hummel, which were practically commandeered for the exclusive use of the military. Nevertheless, the town remained quiet in late 1861 and 1862 except for a conspiracy started by General E.A. Paine to oust General C.F. Smith during the Battle of Belmont, a raid by Grant on the Confederate camp opposite Fort De Russey at Columbus on November 7, 1861.

Paine had ignored explicit orders from General Smith and had been reprimanded. The political appointee seethed. Not long after Smith had reprimanded Paine at the Battle of Belmont, a letter from an irate citizen at Paducah accused Smith of being "soft" on rebels. The writer felt that Smith should confiscate provisions and materials going to rebel sympathizers instead of observing the contraband laws and complained that Smith protects "rebels whilst union men suffer—and the soldiers [are] ready to rise against his policy."

Paducah was not accustomed to the parade ground discipline insisted upon by C.F. Smith. Others did not understand Smith's letter-of-the-law approach to rebels and their sympathizers. On one occasion, Smith did give comfort to a rebel. Union troops noticed a rebel flag flying at 631 Kentucky Avenue (formerly the house owned by Lloyd Tilghman, now occupied by Robert Owen Woolfolk). Confederate officers were in town under a flag of truce to arrange an exchange of wounded and were staying with Woolfolk. Aides of General Lew Wallace (the author of *Ben Hur*) tore the rebel flag to pieces and ran up the Union banner. C.F. Smith sent his aide to intervene to assure that the terms of the flag of truce were respected. In one account, Wallace's aide got into a fistfight with Smith's aide and knocked out Smith's man.

LEFT: *General Lew Wallace penned* Ben Hur *after the end of the Civil War.*
RIGHT: *A native Kentuckian, General J.T. Boyle became commander of the Department of Kentucky in 1862. He immediately offended many Kentuckians by arresting those suspected of Southern sentiments. (Courtesy Kentucky Historical Society, Frankfort.)*

Smith felt he knew the source of the rumors. They were the work of "a poor devil as a man or as a soldier by the name of Paine." Smith accused Paine of trying to oust him from the command at Paducah. In this Paine did not succeed at all. Henry Wager Halleck, "Old Brains," who replaced Frémont at St. Louis, backed Smith and sent Paine to Bird's Point near Cairo to commune with the ducks.

Early in 1862, Grant started the campaign that eventually cost the South use of the Mississippi and perhaps the war. The first objective was the poorly constructed fort on the Tennessee River near the border. General Lloyd Tilghman of Paducah commanded Fort Henry. This post was poorly planned and placed in a position that was subject to flooding. Guns placed on the higher ground on the opposite shore also could command the fort. Tilghman realized that the post was not defensible; therefore, he sent the bulk of his command to Fort Donelson on the Cumberland River near Dover, Tennessee. Tilghman planned only a token defense against Union gunboats. On February 6, the post fell to the Union ironclads of Andrew Foote. The victorious gunboats came back to Paducah en route to the Cumberland River and Fort Donelson.

During the period February 12-16, Union forces casually approached Fort Donelson, surrounded it, contained an attempt of the garrison to break out, and took the fort. The fall of Forts Henry and Donelson opened the vitals of the Confederacy to penetration by the ironclad gunboats of Grant. The Tennessee River was open to navigation from Paducah to Muscle Shoals, Alabama. Nashville lay on the Cumberland and could not be held. In a short time, the Confederates

The Ed Murray house served as headquarters for General Lew Wallace while he was in Paducah. (Courtesy Dr. William Blalock family.)

The home of Lloyd Tilghman is one of the few pre–Civil War houses in Paducah still in use.

Commodore Foote's Western Fleet approaches Fort Henry in 1862, as shown in this sketch appearing in Leslie's Illustrated.

moved out of their strongholds in Kentucky. Bowling Green and Columbus were abandoned without a fight. Rebel troops also left the pocket they occupied at the Cumberland Gap. The war entered a new phase. The Confederates abandoned Columbus on February 27. The Federals entered and took possession of the "Gibraltar of the West" on March 3.

With the threat of military action removed from the immediate vicinity of Paducah, the town settled down to a more routine life. The city became a staging area for operations south. On April 2, 1862, a storm with powerful winds ravaged part of Paducah. Seventeen stores, hotels, and other structures suffered damage, including the spire of the Methodist church. The same spire had been destroyed by a tornado on August 9, 1851, along with two boats and a hotel, the Marshall House, later called the Richmond House. The *Dover* and the *Caledonia* were sunk. Six other boats were severely damaged.

Four days later, the first massive battle in the west took place at Pittsburgh Landing, or Shiloh. Grant managed to stop an assault by 25,000 Confederates under Kentuckian Albert Sidney Johnston, who bled to death from what should have been a minor wound. Grant lost his hope of a quick victory over the Confederates. War became hell. Resolve hardened. There was no room for tolerance of dissent.

Following the slaughter at Shiloh, Paducah became a vast hospital for sick and wounded soldiers. Several churches, the female seminary, the courthouse, and other buildings were used as infirmaries until the close of the war. One facility pressed into service as a hospital was home to the Episcopalians. The pews were removed and left outside. For some reason, army mules developed the habit of gnawing at the backs of the seats. Perhaps it was the sweat of saints and sinners that attracted the animals. The marks reminded the members of the event years afterward. When the pews were replaced, the older ones went to an African-American congregation.

Grant's move down the Tennessee and Cumberland Rivers proved decisive. Eventually, Vicksburg was taken and the Mississippi opened. The South was split and all that remained was that it be squeezed to death, following General Winfield Scott's Anaconda Plan.

6. The Reign of Terror

Following the fall of Forts Henry and Donelson, the Confederacy left Kentucky. Grant began a relentless pursuit that was to displace rebels from Tennessee, Mississippi, and Georgia. At times, the South would lash back, like at Shiloh, only to be defeated and driven inexorably from city to city and from state to state. The farther south the armies of the Cumberland and the Tennessee pushed their Confederate counterparts, the more important it became to find some way to divert the Union from its primary objective—the destruction of the heart of the Confederacy.

In 1862, Braxton Bragg led a Confederate army into Kentucky following the Louisville & Nashville Railroad north. Don Carlos Buell managed to get his Union troops back from Tennessee and imposed them between Bragg and Louisville. Rather than risk a major engagement, Bragg drifted back toward Tennessee before heading northeast, pausing to fight the only engagement in Kentucky in which the main lines of rival armies clashed. The Battle of Perryville started on October 8 and thwarted the plans of Bragg to recruit and recover Kentucky for the rebel cause. Bragg hoped to recruit 20,000 Kentuckians and had brought wagonloads of uniforms in expectation. Only about 2,500 showed up to enlist. Bragg railed at the Kentuckians, saying "Why then should I stay with my handful of brave Southern men to fight for cowards who sulked about in the dark to say to us, 'We are with you, only whip these fellows out of our country, and let us see you can protect us, and we will join you.'" Afterwards, many in Kentucky detested the memory of Bragg.

No other major Confederate invasion occurred; however, John Hunt Morgan and Nathan Bedford Forrest did lead raids into Kentucky in 1864 and 1865. Federal policy changed as a result of these incursions. Garrisons kept towns and defended railroad lines. The interior was left alone. As a result, guerrilla warfare with bands of regulars cut off from their commands, deserters, and bandits erupted throughout Kentucky. Efforts by the military to break up such irregular gangs failed due to a lack of cavalry. This led to a progressive increase in repression of the civilian population.

By a strange twist, Jews were among the first to suffer persecution from the military. The role of the Jewish population in Paducah differs from that in many other cities. Not only have the Germans and Jews from Germany formed a welcomed part of the leadership in the business community of the town from very early times, but one of the mayors serving the longest span in that office in Paducah was a German Jew, Meyer Weil (who served four terms—1871, 1873, 1875, and 1877). Weil came to Paducah in 1863 and set up in the tobacco and brokerage business. Perhaps the reaction to Yankee persecution helped foster the sympathetic attitude toward Paducah Jews.

General Order Eleven, issued December 17, 1862, at Holly Springs, is a milestone in anti-Semitism by an agent of the government of the United States:

> The Jews, as a class violating every regulation of trade established by the Treasury Department and also department orders, are hereby expelled from the department within twenty-four hours from receipt of this order. Post commanders will see that all of this class of people be furnished passes and required to leave and any one returning after such notification will be arrested and held in confinement until an opportunity occurs of sending them out as prisoners, unless furnished with permit from headquarters. No passes will be given these people to visit headquarters for the purpose of making personal application for trade permits.

Among those sent to Cincinnati from Paducah were J.W. Kaskel, David Wolff, and Caesar Kaskel. The three Paducahans registered their protest with Congressman Gurley of Ohio, who appealed to the President: "We respectfully ask your immediate attention to this enormous outrage on all law and humanity, and pray for your effectual and immediate interposition." Lincoln had the order rescinded.

General Halleck told Grant why Lincoln overruled his order. "The President has no objection to your expelling traitors and Jew Peddlers, which, I suppose, was the object of your order; but, as its terms proscribe an entire religious class, some of whom are fighting in our ranks, the President deemed it necessary to revoke it."

Among the Jewish community in Paducah today there is a tradition that tells how citizens of Paducah hid Jews to prevent their being sent to some army camp. One soldier is said to have knocked on the door of a Jew and demanded, "What are you?" The resident of the house answered truthfully, "Tailor." To which the soldier replied, "Sorry to bother you, Mr. Taylor, but I'm looking for Jews."

During 1862, efforts were made by Federal officials to assure the election of those in sympathy with the Union (Republican) objectives. On July 21 at Louisville, General Jerry Boyle issued General Order Five: "No person hostile in opinion to the government and desiring its overthrow, will be allowed to stand for office in the district of Kentucky." This order was instrumental in achieving the election of R.K. Williams of Paducah to the Court of Appeals for the Fourth District; however, other candidates did not fare as well. The voter turnout was quite light. Union ticket supporters won everywhere because the decision to allow a person to vote was not determined by the state's election officials but by

Caesar Kaskel of Paducah (seen here) and Congressman Gurley of Ohio took the protest of the expulsion of Jews by U.S. Grant to Washington, D.C. and President Lincoln. The order was rescinded. (Courtesy Temple Israel.)

the military. Officials of the state protested violation of their constitutional rights as a loyal state.

Governor Magoffin detailed election irregularities in his report to the legislature issued August 15, 1862. These documents include correspondence between Circuit Judge Wiley P. Fowler of Smithland, County Judge G.A. Flournoy, County Clerk Thomas D. Grundy of McCracken County, and Colonel S. Noble, commanding the United States Army at Paducah. The governor itemized the gross disregard of the rights of state officials by the military.

At issue was an oath. Noble wrote Fowler, "Officers of your court in different counties are secessionists, and have not taken the oath of allegiance." He further claimed that these same men were "oppressing Union men and talking treason in the very presence of the court." Noble lectured Fowler by pointing out that "the Union army came here to sustain and defend the constitution of the United States, to protect Union men, and punish treason wherever it may be found, whether in high or low places." To comply with the regulations, Fowler must ensure that all jurors, both grand and petit, should take the oath before being impaneled. Noble concluded, "I want a record of such oath sent to these headquarters."

However, Fowler "refused to comply with the order, declining to yield to any dictation by military authority as to the discharge of his duties as presiding officer of the court, and ordered an immediate adjournment until court in course," according to Richard Collins's *History of Kentucky*. Magoffin concurred with the conduct of Fowler on May 20: "For the dignity of the bench, for the honor of the state. And in the name of the liberties of our people, I hope you will pay no attention to the illegal, unconstitutional, and tyrannical action." In fact, Magoffin advised Fowler not to appear as ordered at Paducah. Fowler did appear on May 23.

Noble also held Flournoy and Grundy to the same oath requirement. They told the colonel that they had taken all the oaths necessary and required by the laws of Kentucky. They were denied the exercise of their offices. Magoffin protested this action to John J. Crittenden in Washington and the senator took the matter up with the secretary of war. On June 7, Crittenden was informed that General Halleck would "investigate and report." Nothing came of this.

The tenth document Magoffin sent to the legislature was a letter from J. Bigger, a Paducah attorney. The letter, dated July 8, 1862, complained that Bigger was denied his right to hold public office under the Kentucky Constitution:

> On this morning an order was presented to me purporting to have been issued from the office of the provost marshal at this place, by command of Brig. Gen. Boyle, directing me to decline the office of circuit judge of the first judicial district, and upon my failure to comply, I am informed that I will be reported under arrest to headquarters United States forces at Louisville, Ky.

The year 1864 proved to be a dramatic one for Paducah. Union recruiters began to enroll African Americans despite the opposition of Kentuckians. On July 8, 1863, the U.S. War Department authorized the enlistment of free blacks into the armed forces. A strong protest from Kentucky caused Lincoln to agree on October 25 not to enlist free blacks in Kentucky as long as sufficient whites met the state's quotas. Publication of the Emancipation Proclamation earlier that year did not affect slavery in Kentucky, as it only applied to the territory then under Union

Q.Q. Quigley recorded his keen observations of events in Paducah during the days leading up to the Civil War and the days after. (Courtesy George Langstaff.)

control of states in rebellion. Even so, residents of Paducah were shocked at the thought of freeing slaves.

Q.Q. Quigley noted the announcement in his *Journal* for Wednesday, January 7, 1863: "President Lincoln issued his proclamation on the 1st instant declaring all the Negroes free except in the State of Kentucky, Tennessee, Maryland, Missouri, Western Virginia, and a few parishes in Louisiana and a few counties in Virginia." Quigley felt this act was "the blackest act . . . ever done by Christian man." Quigley accepted the "natural state" for the African American as that assigned to Ham in the Bible as "hewers of wood and drawers of water." Quigley felt the act was unfair to blacks, as "None of the rules of civilized warfare will be applied to him but execution, fire, and the sword."

Early in 1864, the Union position on slavery in loyal states changed 180 degrees. The adjutant general of the Union Army, Lorenzo Thomas, arrived in Paducah and telegraphed Secretary of War Edwin Stanton: "I arrived here this morning. In my letter of the 1st instant, I reported instructions respecting the First Artillery Regiment Colored Troops, to be raised at Paducah, Kentucky. Shall I proceed with its organization?" By the end of the war, two African-American artillery regiments and parts of several African-American infantry regiments had been recruited at Paducah. Enlistment in the armed forces freed a slave and his family. Enlistment also meant a high risk since soldiers in the black units had exceedingly high death rates. The major threat was exposure to various diseases. However, in 1864, a Confederate officer, Colonel W.P. Shingler, told his subordinates "not to report the capture of any more Negroes."

The death rate of the African-American regiment at Paducah was over twice that of most white units, perhaps due to exposure to communicable diseases for the first time. Here are numbers for the U.S. 8th Artillery:

Company	No. Listed	Died	KIA	Discharged	Transferred
A	110	37	0	16	19
B	114	36	0	11	1
C	91	46	2	15	5
D	88	46	0	0	0
E	89	46	0	8	36
F	86	31	0	10	0
G	91	31	0	16	1
H	102	42	0	10	0
I	109	41	0	4	0
K	91	50	0	11	0
L	58	27	0	9	0

The use of African Americans as soldiers was not popular in Kentucky, especially in the far western part of the state. On March 21, 1864, Colonel Richard L. Cunningham of the 8th U.S. Heavy Artillery sent some of his black soldiers at Paducah to recruit black deck hands off the steamer *Carrie Jacobs*.

The officers and crew of the boat resisted and appealed to white soldiers nearby for help. A fight ensued between blacks and whites and several were reported seriously injured on each side. There was no similar incident when whites were recruited for the Union at Paducah.

George F. Barnes started recruiting whites for the 16th Kentucky Cavalry on February 15, 1864. John E. Williamson, E.J. Pendrick, H.H. Hamilton, and S.B. McAfee assisted Barnes (later this outfit became a part of the 12th Kentucky cavalry). The unit was still raw and untested when it was called upon to help defend Paducah against an attack by other Paducahans in the second crisis of 1864.

Nathan Bedford Forrest sent Abraham Buford's Kentuckians (including many from the Purchase area) north toward Paducah in an attempt to relieve the hard-pressed Confederate army fighting before Atlanta. The goal of the raid was to cut the vital supply lines running through Kentucky. Captain H.A. Taylor led the advance with his company of the 12th Kentucky, CSA. Federal pickets were encountered 3 or 4 miles from the city of Paducah and were pushed back in upon their fortifications. The Federal forces, led by Colonel S.G. Hicks of Illinois, consisted of the 122nd Illinois Infantry, 16th Kentucky Cavalry, and 1st Kentucky Artillery plus the 8th U.S. Heavy Artillery. The Federals withdrew into Fort Anderson, where they were supported by fire from the gunboats *Peosta* and *Paw-Paw*.

Louis Kolb Sr. recalled the Battle of Paducah in an article in the *News-Democrat* on March 25, 1927, 63 years after the battle took place. The advanced rebel contingent arrived at the Union outpost at Eden's Hill about 2:10 Saturday afternoon. By 3:00 p.m., Forrest's main body reached what is now Fifteenth and Broadway, where they dismounted to wait for dark. Kolb and his young wife got to "the river bank about 5 o'clock, on the afternoon of the battle." Kolb managed to gain a place for his family in a small boat. "I clung fast to the bottom of the boat while the firing was going on, near a woman with a bad case of smallpox, having less fear of contracting the disease than the shots from in and around the fort." The Kolbs crossed over the Ohio to Brookport, where they remained until the fighting ended on Sunday.

As soon as the Confederates came within cannon-shot, the guns in the fort opened up on them. A participant recalled, "The Kentuckians were dismounted and moved in line of battle in the direction of the fort. The alignment was maintained until the more densely built-up portion of the city was reached, when it was broken by the buildings and the further advance had to be made along the streets in column by regiments or companies." The Confederates halted for a short time about 300 yards from the enemy and protected themselves by getting behind houses in the street and alleys that ran at right angles to those leading out in the direction of the fort. Harvey George, in the *History of the 3rd, 7th, 8th, and 12th Kentucky C.S.A.* wrote the following:

> While marching through the streets the command was under a constant and withering fire from the fort by both small arms and artillery.

> When out in the open space, the lines were somewhat adjusted before the final charge was made. When within a short distance of the fort it was discovered that it was surrounded by a deep ditch with such perpendicular banks as to render crossing impossible.

At that, a retreat was ordered back to cover of the buildings. There, "a terrific fire was kept up on the fort until near night at which time the whole command was withdrawn a short distance from the city and went into camp for the night," according to George.

Forrest is generally considered to be one of the most effective leaders on either side in the war. However, the attack on Fort Anderson does little to enhance his reputation. Perhaps Forrest counted too much on the lack of training of the Federals. Perhaps he acceded too quickly to the demands of the Paducah personnel who wanted to impress the home folks, or perhaps he felt that sheer audacity would carry the day. For whatever reason, Forrest did not make a proper reconnaissance. The ditch should not have been a surprise. Of this engagement, Forrest said, "I drove the enemy to their gunboats and fort, and held the town for ten hours; captured many stores and horses; burned sixty bales of cotton, one steamer and a dry-dock, bringing out fifty prisoners. My loss, as far as known, is twenty-five killed and wounded, among them Colonel Thompson." A.P. Thompson had been given command of the brigade to allow him the honor of

USS Peosta, *along with the USS* Paw Paw, *aided in the defense of Fort Anderson against two attacks by forces of Nathan Bedford Forrest in 1864. (Courtesy U.S. Navy Museum, Washington, D.C.)*

taking his hometown. He was killed instantly by a cannon ball while leading his troops in the approach to the fort. Colonel Edward Crossland took over only to be severely wounded. The Union losses were 14 killed, 46 wounded, and 40 prisoners.

Forrest moved back to Mayfield the morning after the raid, and the Kentuckians in his command disbanded for a few days so that they might visit their homes. It is to their everlasting credit to note that they did not abuse this first opportunity since 1861 to see kith and kin. All returned to their command at the appointed time. They also procured fresh mounts and comfortable clothing in addition to recruiting a number of new volunteers, which brought the regiments up to something like their proper size again.

Paducah suffered considerable damage, both by the raiders in their deliberate destruction of military stores and by the defenders in their efforts to defend Fort Anderson. Union headquarters, quartermaster, and commissary buildings with all stores, the steamboat *Dacotah*, and the railroad depot were put to the torch. The defenders burned all houses near the fort to prevent their being used again to shelter an attacking party.

Forrest was not finished with the Purchase. He had unsuccessfully attacked Fort Anderson (with its African-American defenders as one possible target), but another opportunity soon presented itself to impress on the black population the danger of taking up arms against the Confederacy. This was the massacre at Fort Pillow, Tennessee, where the Union garrison surrendered only to have the African-American troopers shot, driven into the Mississippi, or buried alive in one or two instances. Had Fort Anderson capitulated, the same fate could have awaited its black contingent.

Forrest let the Kentuckians in his command attack Fort Anderson, as their former slaves were among those in the garrison. At Fort Pillow, Forrest sent his Kentucky troops on furlough and let the Tennessee and Mississippi troopers have the honor of taking the fort and dealing with the former slaves. A former slave dealer from Memphis, "Forrest at Paducah . . . indicated that if he must storm the works 'no quarter' would be shown the Negro troops." Forrest did send a flag of truce to Fort Anderson informing Colonel Hicks that he had no choice but to surrender or be stormed. Colonel Hicks had been severely wounded at Shiloh and was not cowed by Forrest's threat. Instead, Hicks informed Forrest that he meant to do his duty. Three attacks were repulsed.

The vacationing Kentuckians of Forrest's command came together at Trenton, Tennessee, by the first part of April 1864. Forrest ordered General Buford to take them back into Western Kentucky for two purposes: "First, to direct the attention of the Federal commanders away from Fort Pillow, which Forrest planned to take, secondly, to capture a lot of good horses and mules that were reported to be in the suburbs of Paducah."

Buford sent Captain H.A. Taylor with about 110 men to make a demonstration before Columbus to pin that garrison within the fortifications while the main body raided Paducah. Taylor was so successful that the Union commander at

Considered one of the most effective leaders in the Civil War, Nathan Bedford Forrest, CSA, raided Paducah twice.

Columbus thought he was under attack by the complete command of Forrest. Buford arrived at Paducah on the morning of the 14th and made a great flurry of movement, driving the garrison back into Fort Anderson and onto the gunboats. The Union garrison remained pinned down by a few men while Buford's men gathered up about 200 animals that had been overlooked during their first visit. After procuring the horses, Buford leisurely moved his command back to Trenton, giving some men additional furloughs on the way.

Popular support of the Confederates under Forrest during the two raids caused Union commanders to demand harsher measures to suppress Southern sentiment. Prior to Forrest's raids in 1864, the Treasury Department had removed all restrictions on trade in Kentucky and Missouri. Immediately after the two incursions, the Federal commander at Cairo complained to General Grant that "goods going from Cairo, Paducah and Hickman will undoubtedly reach Tennessee if unrestricted, as I have not sufficient force to guard the whole border." This soon proved to be the state of affairs. Federal officials claimed that the railroad line between Paducah to Mayfield and the stretch between Columbus and Union City, Tennessee, were used to transport goods to the Confederacy. This was distressing, as Forrest was still in that area and his cavalry benefited from this illegal traffic. The commander at Cairo acknowledged, "for the past few months the interior of Western Kentucky has been filled with war-like stores and army supplies of every kind." He blamed the situation on "the loose administration of the Treasury and Army officials."

The Federal commander at Cairo finally felt compelled to take the initiative. On April 2, he issued a general order forbidding steamboats from landing between

Paducah and Memphis. In addition, he halted the use of all ferryboats, trading boats, skiffs, or other small craft operating on the Ohio and the Mississippi Rivers in this area. All traffic out of Paducah and Columbus was prohibited except for military purposes. The Treasury approved this action on April 13. However, not all complaints came from the military. A group of Paducah merchants calling themselves the "Union League of America" protested that the "rebels are doing all the business, and they are reaping all the advantages of trade."

The two raids by Forrest in March through Western Kentucky and the sweeps through the center of the state by Morgan during the first part of June heartened the faltering rebel supporters and caused an increase in guerrilla depredations. The ease and frequency of the incursions of Confederate regulars, coupled with the mounting boldness of the irregulars, caused General Elihu B. Washburne, commanding the district of West Tennessee, which included that part of Kentucky west of the Cumberland River, to issue an order that "the people of that disloyal region, Western Kentucky, will not be allowed to sell their cotton and tobacco, or purchase supplies, unless they show some friendship for the United States government, by driving out the guerrillas and irregular bands of Confederate soldiers who pay them frequent visits."

On July 5, President Lincoln was so alarmed at the deterioration of the situation in Kentucky that he acted unilaterally. The writ of habeas corpus was suspended and martial law was proclaimed. From this date on, the fate of people suspected of supporting the South hinged upon the caprices of military commanders. Eleven days later, General Order No. 59 of General Stephen Burbridge provided

"General Pain"—General Eleazar A. Paine of Illinois—proved to be troublesome to many residents of Paducah.

that all rebel sympathizers living within 5 miles of a guerrilla outrage should be arrested and deported beyond the limits of the United States and their property seized in sufficient quantity to repay for losses arising from enemy action. For every unarmed Union citizen killed by guerrillas, four guerrilla prisoners should be taken from the nearest military prison and shot at a spot conveniently near the outrage.

E.A. Paine assumed command at Paducah on July 19, 1864, and began a 51-day "reign of terror." Paine declared that only loyal people would be allowed to trade. To enforce this decision, he levied "a tax of $10 on every hogshead of tobacco or bale of cotton, and a tax assessment of 25 percent *ad valorum* on all cotton which had ever been the property of a disloyal person."

On August 1, Paine levied a tax of $100,000 on residents of his military district to be collected from "persons known to be or suspected of being Confederate sympathizers." In addition, "heavy sums were paid for [trade] permits, which, if admissible, should have been freely granted, and, if improper, should have . . . been refused." These trade permits had been authorized by General Order No. 63 of General Burbridge on August 13, which absolutely interdicted all shipments of produce or goods of any kind, either in, or through, or into the state—except upon a permit, issued for four months, to persons of "well known loyalty," whose status was determined "by a board of five advisors, well known citizens of unquestionable loyalty, respectability, and integrity, and who, in case of doubt, will be bound by an oath." Should irregularities occur, the parties would be arrested and imprisoned and the military authorities would seize their trade goods.

On October 26, Burbridge published General Order No. 8, which provided that "hereafter, no guerrilla will be received as prisoners, and any officer who may capture such, and extend to them the courtesies due to prisoners of war, will be held accountable for disobedience of orders." This did not stop guerrilla raids and most of Western Kentucky remained unsettled until the end of the war. Even the Confederates took notice of such irregular operations. Burbridge was a Radical Republican and regarded any Democrat as a closet rebel.

Bank checks were not to pass unless they had the approval of Paine or one of his agents. The privilege of using bank drafts now cost 50¢ each. A standing charge of 10¢ was made on all letters, newspapers, or packages that left Paducah. In some instances, such as the case of African-American soldiers in the Union garrison, 50¢ was charged for permission to send letters to relatives. John Sauner, the mayor of Paducah from 1859 until 1863, received orders to appear before General Paine. Upon arriving, Paine proceeded to "cuss him out" for about an hour. "General," replied Sauner, "if I were on equal terms, you couldn't call me those names." Paine then ordered the guard to shoot Sauner if he got in the general's way. Sauner took the hint and left Paducah on the next boat to Cincinnati and did not return until after the departure of Paine. John Fisher, a German loyal to the Union, was mayor during this incident. The city records mention the incident and blame "General Pain." It is likely the clerk knew how to spell the general's name.

Determined to punish those giving aid to the enemy, Paine mounted intense pressure to demoralize those known to favor the Confederacy. The *Detroit Free Press* for August 11, 1864, reported the arrival in that city of a party from Columbus, Paducah, and vicinity en route to Canada. They had been banished from the United States on orders of General Paine for "giving aid and comfort to the enemy." Paine determined to send them to hell, Canada, or Africa.

According to the newspaper, the group was under the supervision of Captain B.H. Norton, 8th U.S. Heavy Artillery, "and the fragrance of about two dozen artillerists." On August 8, the detachment of African-American soldiers left Paducah and added the group from Columbus before proceeding in a closed train to the border at Detroit. Among those from Columbus was William McKeene Hubbard, who kept a diary of the experience:

> The following persons were banished by order of Brigadier General Paine from Columbus, Ky., July 31, 1864: James P. Walker, Burn M. Walker, Joe M. Moore, T.M. Moore, T.M. Horne, Mrs. Josephine Overall, Wm. McKeene Hubbard, Judge W.R. Vance [former mayor of Louisville], Robert E. Cook, Jas. Morton, Geor. B. Moss, Chas. Rickee, John Glenn, W.G. Malone, wife and six children, in all twenty-one persons. We were allowed from Sunday the 31st of July to Monday morning, the 8th of August, to close up our books, wind up our businesses and prepare for banishment. On Sunday night, the 7th, the following assessments were levied by Gen. Paine's orders: Wm. McKeene Hubbard, $1,000, paid; J.P. and B.M. Walker, $5,000, not paid; Jas. Morton, $5,000, not paid.

According to Hubbard, "those who were exiled were among the most prominent people of Columbus." He remembered that he paid his fine as he considered himself a loyal citizen and proposed to abide by the laws of the land. He was the only one who paid. As a result, some, like the Malone family, had their property confiscated until their return from exile.

The Paducahans included Mrs. Robert Woolfolk and six children, Mrs. Rollston, Kate Saunders, Mrs. Joe Sam Hobbs, Robert Shanklin, and others in a party reported to number between 18 and 20.

Despite the rigid censorship Paine exercised through the control of the telegraph and the mail leaving the city, word of the situation reached Jesse J. Craddock of the First Regiment of Capital Guards at Frankfort, who sent a petition to General Burbridge. As a result, Brigadier Speed Smith and Colonel John Mason Brown went to Paducah to conduct an investigation into the conduct of Paine. Before the commission arrived, Paine and others fled to Illinois with all the general's records. The investigators found a mess. In its report, the commission furnished sworn testimony to the effect that Lucien Anderson, (congressman of the First District), John F. Bollinger, R.H. Hall (provost marshal), Major Henry Bartling (8th U.S. Heavy Artillery), and Thomas M. Redd (surveyor of the port of

Paducah) were involved in various acts of corruption, bribery, gross malfeasance, and oppression of the population of Paducah. Others also were cited for acts equally shocking.

The first act of Brigadier S. Meredith upon assuming command at Paducah was to release 51 prisoners at Mayfield and to empty the guardhouse at Paducah. The reign of terror was over; however, Kentuckians still were not secure. An exchange of letters between Governor Thomas Bramlette of Kentucky and President Lincoln, between Bramlette and General Burbridge, and between Lincoln and Burbridge resulted. On January 8, 1865, Lincoln set aside the order of Burbridge that restricted all trade with Kentucky. Finally, to rid himself of the constant squabbles in Kentucky, Lincoln placed Major General John Palmer in command. Most Kentuckians agreed with the *Louisville Journal* and rejoiced with "thanks God and President Lincoln."

Q.Q. Quigley had not made an entry in his diary since June 26, 1863. He resumed his writing on November 11, 1865. "Once again I feel that I may safely open up my book and make it once more the companion of my thoughts. No more do I hide it for fear that the vandal eyes of Paine's detectives may search it out and henceforth I will hold communication with it." He did not intend to reconstruct his thoughts over the blank interval, "For the most that would result to me would be the revival of hates and contempts for men and states that had as well be forgotten." Paducahans, like Quigley, were ready to accept the status quo and get on with their lives.

This statue of Confederate Brigadier General Lloyd Tilghman stands in Paducah's Lang Park in memory of this soldier and the city's Civil War heritage.

7. Reunion and Rebuilding

The end of the Civil War found Paducah, like many other cities in Kentucky, facing the problem of reabsorbing that part of its population that had fought for either the South or the North and creating a place in society for that part of the population that had been considered chattel. Patterns of commerce disrupted during the war had to be renewed and realigned. Later, in the period following the depression of 1873, default and debt became specters haunting the city. Still, Paducah weathered the series of crises and emerged strong and vibrant.

Confederate veterans wanted to return to their homes in Kentucky at the end of hostilities; however, many feared that they would be subject to the terms of the existing laws that threatened them with trial on charges ranging from felonies to misdemeanors. General Palmer took the lead in easing the reception of the returning rebels. He let it be known that those willing to make a personal surrender, give up arms and horse, and register with the military would be allowed to return in peace.

During the state elections held in August 1865, General Palmer used Federal troops at the polls to dissuade voters from supporting candidates other than those favorable to the Radical Republican program. Many Kentuckians considered the presence of African-American soldiers in a state that still recognized slavery as a legal institution a flagrant insult. In *The Civil War and Reconstruction in Kentucky*, Ellis M. Coulter wrote that General Palmer "cost the Union party 10,000 votes in this State." The immediate response was the election of a legislature that was disposed to favor the returning rebels. Perhaps as a partial response to Palmer's actions, act after act removed restrictions of all kinds from returning Confederates.

By the end of February 1866, former Confederates could return to Paducah at will. Members of the various companies of the 3rd Kentucky, CSA (including Company "D" that was known as "the Paducah Company") met a friendlier welcome than on their previous visit. For them, life soon returned to normal. This was not the case for the city, however. It had to make amends for one exhibition of Southern enthusiasm early in the war.

Owners of the *Samuel Orr*, the river packet seized by the citizens of Paducah in 1861 and sent to the Confederacy in retaliation for the confiscation of the *W.B. Terry* by the U.S. Navy, brought suit against the City in federal district court to recover damages. The City agreed to compromise and paid the William McClurg, Kahn, and Longacker Company, the plaintiff, a total of $30,000 in damages.

Returning Confederates quickly blended into Paducah society. Charles Reed served with General Lloyd Tilghman, fought at Shiloh, and participated in the two raids on Paducah. After coming back to Paducah, he managed hotels and served four successive two-year terms as mayor, from 1881 to 1889. (Courtesy McCPL.)

The end of the war did not end slavery in Kentucky. The commonwealth insisted upon its right to maintain property in chattel up to the very end. In fact, Kentucky did not ratify the Thirteenth Amendment ending the "peculiar institution" and haughtily rejected any suggestion that the state should anticipate the inevitable and abolish slavery voluntarily. State officials had sworn to uphold the state constitution and they meant to do so, even if the result was open conflict with Federal officials such as John M. Palmer, who was equally determined to abolish slavery by any means. Each side recognized the futility of any effort to preserve slavery, yet each party acted in accord with the dictates of conscience. The slave was caught between state's rights and the sovereignty of the federal government. Kentucky finally ratified the Thirteenth, Fourteenth, and Fifteenth Amendments in 1976 as a gesture of goodwill during the bicentennial of the Declaration of Independence.

The Constitution of Kentucky prohibited freeing slaves without the consent of their owners. Further, if a slave was freed, he had to leave the state or face legal action. On July 17, 1862, Congress passed a law freeing slaves of rebels if the slaves enlisted in labor units. The Proclamation of Emancipation of January 1, 1863, did not provide for compensation of slaveowners. As it only applied to rebel states, Kentucky was exempt from its provisions; however, the measure did present the prospect of future loss of property. Kentucky responded by passing a law denying entry to freed men from states farther south on March 2, 1863.

In 1863, the Union allowed the enlistment of free blacks. Lincoln excluded Kentucky, but as the war progressed, it became obvious that African Americans could help win the war. On March 3, 1865, the slaves in Kentucky who enlisted in the Federal forces were freed and so were their families. Palmer used this law to free many slaves in Kentucky after the fighting stopped—much to the dismay of the Kentucky officials. Nor would Palmer allow Kentucky officials to expel the freedmen. Controlling the rail and water routes helped the military enforce its will, and state officials had to omit enforcement of the state law regarding freedmen.

Under the protection of the military, freedmen flocked to the cities. State laws did not apply to the freedmen. This pattern was perpetuated with the inclusion of Kentucky with other slave states under the jurisdiction of the Freedman's Bureau in December 1865. An office opened at Paducah and was to oversee the transformation of the freedmen from property into citizens. Officials of Kentucky felt that their state should not be included in the application of the Freedman's Bureau. Nevertheless, all disputes involving Kentucky blacks now were heard in the bureau courts rather than in the regular tribunals of the state. Thus, the

Blacks in Paducah after the end of slavery were free but their situation had not changed a great deal. Although some African Americans did make significant gains, both socially and economically (as seen in the left portrait of Ellen Cartwright), for many, their situation had not changed a great deal (as seen in the right portrait of cook "Aunt Susan"). (Left portrait: courtesy Mary Hammond; right portrait: McCPL.)

slave went from the protection of his/her master to the army and thence to the Freedman's Bureau—all the while maintaining his/her dependency.

One of the first acts of independence of African Americans was to segregate worship. Whites had feared any meeting of slaves without supervision as a potential source for plotting violent uprisings such as that of Nat Turner earlier in Virginia; therefore, slaves either attended church with their owners or met apart with their approval and with at least one white in attendance. Such was the case of the African Baptist Church, which petitioned the City in 1858 to be allowed to hold meetings on alternate nights for two weeks until 10 p.m. with the understanding that some respectable white person was in attendance. A similar request in December was turned down.

With freedom, black preachers began to preach to blacks. One of the more popular preachers was George "Pappy" Dupuy. While a slave of Reverend Craig in Lexington, Dupuy preached to the Pleasant Green Baptist Church. The death of his master in 1847 brought a crisis to the congregation until William M. Pratt, a white Baptist minister, agreed to purchase Dupuy and allow his congregation to redeem him over time. This was done, just in time for freedom. Dupuy then moved to Paducah and changed the African Baptist Church, with its part-time white minister, into the Washington Street Baptist Church, where African Americans could worship without being subject to white supervision.

For black Paducahans in 1865, freedom did not include citizenship, let alone equality. The freedman gained many rights but remained a ward of the federal government under the protection of the Freedman's Bureau and the army. A freedman could not testify in a state court against a white and he certainly was not entitled to vote. Changes soon made both of these possible. Congress passed the Fourteenth Amendment on July 28, 1868, making African Americans citizens despite the rejection of this amendment by Kentucky. The Fifteenth Amendment, passed on March 30, 1870, gave black adult males the right to vote. Again, Kentucky opposed the passage of this measure. By 1872, Kentucky realized that her state government could not hinder the implementation of the new legislation and granted blacks the right to testify in state courts. The wave of lawlessness that followed the Civil War had been curbed by 1872. Regulators and Ku Kluxers used violence to intimidate the black community (as well as an opportunity to settle personal grudges and as a disguise for murder, rape, and robbery). Governor Preston H. Leslie took a tough stand against all marauders upon taking office in September 1871. In this, he was backed by the general assembly.

A new era was in the making. The question was, would African Americans hold the balance of power between the Democratic Party and the Republican Party in Kentucky? The election of 1872 was looked upon as the first real test.

8. INDUSTRY

Paducah originally depended upon merchandising and transportation. As the town grew, it became the center of marketing for agricultural products, particularly dark-fired tobacco. The first industry was related to river transportation, and the local marine ways have remained a valuable contributor to the prosperity of the community. Railroads came in the decade before the Civil War and expanded after the war to become the principal employer in the city and the fourth-largest industry in the state. Manufacturing began with lumber products. Light industry in the hosiery mills came to Paducah in the early years of the twentieth century. Machinery to knit hose was a prized product of Paducah. The advent of heavy industry followed World War II and was located outside the corporate limits of the city. In particular, the construction of the atomic plant produced a major transformation of Paducah.

The first industry in Paducah began with the contract between Elijah Lovejoy of St. Louis and the town. Lovejoy was to receive $1,000 for use of his patented marine rail system and another $500 to supervise the construction of the ways. The agreement was reached on August 25, 1843; however, actual operation did not begin until 1854, when eight rail sections capable of holding boats 350 feet in length were completed. Steamboats and barges were built on these ways.

River transportation played a vital role in the development of Paducah. Passing steamboats could buy wood stacked at the Paducah landing for 12.5¢ per cord in 1833. By 1842, the riverfront was graded and graveled at a cost of $1,000. This made the arrival of the Fowler wharf boat a welcomed asset to the town. Now, steamboats could fuel and take in needed supplies at one stop. After the Civil War, Joe Fowler and others combined with G.C. Grumbaugh to create Fowler Brothers and Company. This organization ran packets on the Ohio, Mississippi, Cumberland, and Tennessee Rivers after the Evansville, Cairo, and Memphis Steam Packet Company in March 1881, and reorganized in 1891. The *Dick Fowler*, a packet of the company, made the one-way trip from Cairo to Evansville in 14 hours and 47 minutes, a record.

Until 1887, the Evansville and Tennessee River Packet Company had a run twice a week from Paducah to Waterloo, Alabama. The later transfer of the mail franchise from river packets to railroads marked the passing of an era.

The aftermath of the 1937 flood proved to be beneficial to river transport. The call for flood control brought forth navigational control as well. Dams on the Ohio

The Seamen's Church Institute trains inland sailors from its location on Water Street.

kept the water level suitable for use even in the summer. River traffic revived in importance to Paducah. With the opening of the Tennessee-Tombigbee canal linking the Tennessee River and the Gulf of Mexico, it is now possible for tows to go directly from Paducah to the Gulf.

As a result, Paducah developed into a central point for the inland water system of more than 25,000 miles of navigable water. More than 3,750 towboats use these waters each year, pushing approximately 21,000 barges containing 1.4 billion metric tons of products annually. A typical inland barge can carry five times its own weight. It has 15 times greater cargo capacity than one rail car and 60 times greater cargo capacity than one semi-trailer.

The increased importance of the inland transport system to Paducah is reflected in one specialized company that provides vital services to the industry. The Center for Maritime Education of the Seamen's Church Institute opened in 1997 and gives specialized training in the navigation of the inland waters to about 800 students annually. The Paducah center is an offshoot of the home location in Brooklyn that trains deep-water mariners. It was founded in 1834 and is affiliated with the Episcopal Church of the United States. The center claims that "Advanced maritime training, aided by simulation, helps professional mariners refine the type of knowledge and proficiency that comes with years of experience and enables them to put that knowledge to work in their careers." The site's simulator can reproduce almost any location of the inland waterway and put the trainees through variable conditions and measure their response. Even the vibrations from the changes in engine speed are felt.

Steamboat Gus Fowler *ran excursions from Paducah. (Courtesy JJ and MHM.)*

Pleasure outings on the Gus Fowler *offered inexpensive entertainment for the whole family (and the dog, too). (Courtesy JJ and MHM.)*

Pictured here are boats under repair in Marine Ways. (Courtesy MHM.)

Lumbering became a mainstay of Paducah from the establishment of the area known as "Jersey" by James Langstaff *c.* 1846 up to 1937. Forty-five acres were purchased in 1847 for $1,200 and a sawmill began operation at the site on lumber brought down the Tennessee River in large rafts. Times were favorable to the new enterprise. More than 100 new houses were erected in Paducah between 1848 and 1849. Jersey began on Island Creek and extended north along present George Street to Sixth and thence west to the creek. The settlement received its name from the fact that Langstaff came from New Jersey.

The area prospered. In May 1849, the firm began the manufacture of the 800,000 bricks needed for the government marine hospital in Paducah. One hundred fifty men worked at the firm at this time.

The Langstaff-Orm Company suffered a major disaster in 1905, when a fire destroyed the sawmill department. Damage was estimated at $20,000 to the equipment, which was steam-driven. The mill had been in constant operation for three weeks at the time of the fire. It had a capacity of 75,000 to 100,000 feet of lumber per day and the firm employed 350 people, about one-half of which were assigned to the mill. The firm rebuilt after the fire, but did not after the flood of 1937, which severely damaged the building and equipment, not to mention the loss of stocks of lumber that floated away. The firm closed in 1939.

The location of a large lumber mill at Paducah helped other firms choose the town for the location of other wood-related products. The Paducah Furniture Manufacturing Company incorporated in 1870 with a stock of $35,000. Elbridge Palmer served as the president and Charles H. Reike Jr. was manager. The firm employed about 100 men and kept 4 salesmen in the field at one time.

This broom factory is an example of a labor-intensive light industry found in Paducah prior to 1900. (Courtesy MHM.)

John W. Little gave his name to a part of Paducah (Littleville) when he decided to move his spoke factory from Dresden, Tennessee, late in 1894. The Tennessee site only had one railroad, and Little felt his company was at the mercy of whatever rate the carrier wanted to impose. At the Paducah location, both the Paducah, Tennessee & Alabama and the Chesapeake, Ohio & Southwestern lines would have to compete in price. Little could reduce his shipping costs. Little employed between 100 and 150 men. When fire destroyed the main building of the company in 1907, city firemen had difficulty fighting it. The building was just in the city limits and the firemen had to run hoses 500 feet to reach the nearest hydrant.

Mechanicsburg, a section of Paducah that adjoins Jersey and runs from the river to the Benton Road, had sawmills, furniture factories, and other plants based upon wood. The McKinnie Veneer and Lumber Company ran a large operation in this section of town around 1900. On April 28, 1897, a raft containing 335,000 feet of prime timber out of Tennessee landed at the mouth of Clark's River. Most of the logs were oak and poplar and one was 12 feet long and 8 feet, 2 inches thick. The McKinnie Veneer and Lumber Company burned on September 27, 1906. Another effort was made to revive the firm at a location at Third and Elizabeth Streets, but that structure burned as well on June 25, 1907.

Another major employer in the Mechanicsburg community was the Mergenthaler-Horton Basket Company. The firm opened in 1902, suffered fire damage, and eventually went bankrupt. At one time 300 people worked for this concern. It had 115 machines designed by Mergenthaler and Emment Horton. Each machine could produce 2,500 baskets for $4.50 less than if they had been made by hand.

Also in the Mechanicsburg section, the Hollingshead Barrel Factory opened in 1901. Its estimated capacity was 2,000 barrels per day with a full complement of 200 workers. The firm supplied barrels to the Gregory Vinegar Works of Paducah (about 20,000 per year). The barrel firm decided to come to Paducah at the urging of the Commerce Club, a local organization that preceded the chamber of commerce as an active agent for searching out additional industries for the city.

E.O. Davis of Paducah got a patent on an attachment for looping machines used in the hosiery industry in 1906. Later, he acquired rights to another patent from William C. Wright of Cleveland, Ohio, and these inventions became the basis for the formation of Southern Textile Company in 1909. This firm produced the machinery used to manufacture women's hose in 44 countries until 1932, when the patent expired. The original plant was located in a remodeled church building at 431 South Third Street. Another facility opened at First and Norton in 1927 in a structure acquired from the Lack Singletree Company for 120 shares of stock. The presence of Southern Textile also led to the formation of Claussner Hosiery Company in 1922 at Second and Adams Streets. Later, a "throwing mill" was

Southern Textile made machinery to knit hosiery for plants around the world, including Claussner Hosiery Company, which produced stockings in Paducah. (Courtesy MHM.)

added at Eleventh and Jefferson. Finally, a large plant was built at Twenty-eighth and Adams, which operated until 1978.

The economic downturn of 1907 caused many of the industries of Paducah to fail, particularly those located in Mechanicsburg. A pool of unemployed workers attracted a new type of enterprise to the community. The firms opening plants in the city of Paducah between 1907 and 1940 were marginal. That is, they were high-cost and low-profit enterprises such as hosiery mills. The success of these firms depended on low wages. As a result, when the operators of these firms gained positions of importance in civic groups such as the Commerce Club, entry of higher-paying firms was discouraged. This attitude helped keep Paducah from growing. Without growth, the city settled into a narrow, self-centered shell. This complacency ended with the advent of the atomic plant.

Paducah became a major market for dark-fired tobacco after the Civil War. Unlike the burley leaf that cures in the open air, this type of tobacco in the Purchase area was cured over slow, smoky fires in a barn. On occasion, the leaf also received a rub of spices and oils that was particularly appealing to the trade with Africa. The tobacco trade also led to an affair that threatened the community.

Paducah has been threatened by outside forces on several occasions: invasion by rival armies, disease, and riders from the Black Patch. The latter refers to a region of Kentucky and Tennessee that produces dark-fired tobacco. Essentially, there are four divisions to the Black Patch: the northern, with markets in Owensboro, Henderson, and Madisonville; the eastern, with markets in Hopkinsville, Princeton, and Clarksville and Springfield, Tennessee; the western, with markets in Mayfield, Murray, Fulton, Paducah, and Paris, Tennessee; and the Bowling Green one-sucker district, with sales at Bowling Green, Glasgow, and Horse Cave.

This is a view of the city market late in the nineteenth century. (MHM.)

William Jackson (wearing a tie) ran the Jackson Foundry in the early 1900s. (Courtesy JSJ.)

Pictured here is the office staff for the Jackson Foundry. (Courtesy JSJ.)

By the end of the nineteenth century, Duke's American Tobacco Trust tried to gain domination in the market for dark-fired tobacco for the domestic market. Two rival groups emerged seeking control over crops in the Black Patch: the Hill Billies, who went along with the trust, and the Night Riders, who banded together in an attempt to gain a better price for their product from the trust or other buyers. All that was needed to become a Night Rider was a horse, a mask, and an alibi. Princeton, Hopkinsville, and Clarksville were occupied by armed bands of Night Riders. Warehouses of the trust were burned at Princeton and Hopkinsville. Anyone opposing the secret army was subjected to terror. If a grower stood against the Night Riders, his plant seedbed would be "scalped" to ensure that no crop would grow.

A pact of silence in Caldwell County assured anyone tried for night riding that a jury of his peers would free him, since most people belonged to the secret society. All Western Kentucky watched the conflict with both dread and admiration. John Miller, attorney for the Hollowells, reported in *The Black Patch Wars*, "even in such a place as Paducah . . . reports of preparation for the raiding of the city by Night Riders had been received, and serious, well grounded apprehension was felt for the safety of the large tobacco warehouses there."

Night Riders had raided Robert Hollowell and his wife, Mary Lou, at their home near Princeton. In the affair, Mrs. Hollowell was shot in the face, receiving minor injuries. A Caldwell County jury heard the case and freed those accused of the attack. The Hollowells left Kentucky and moved to Evansville. There, they entered suit against the Night Riders in the Federal District Court in Paducah. Many feared that the Night Riders might use force to prevent the trial or to intimidate the witnesses. "While the more prominent court officials

The Noble Sand & Gravel Company harvested the rivers at Paducah. (Courtesy McCPL.)

Up to 1950, strawberries were an important crop in Paducah. Carloads of berries were attached to passenger trains and sent to points around the nation. (Courtesy MHM.)

and the leading business people of Paducah were opposed to the Night Riders, and in sympathy with our clients," Miller wrote, "we learned for a certainty that there was in considerable classes a strong undercurrent to the contrary, and in communities within easy striking distance there were organizations that might well be feared." Paducahans anticipated the coming trial with a mixture of apprehension and fascination.

On April 22, 1908, the trial of Robert Hollowell versus his brother John E. Hollowell and 27 others accused of being Night Riders began. The testimony was characterized as sensational, yet nothing new was introduced from the previous trial in the state court. Arguments were completed on April 23. Judge Walter Evans presided, and the jury consisted of the following: W.E. Cochran, George Langstaff, Major T.H. Ashcraft, and James Kroger (Paducah); W.A. Lawrence (Graves County); W.A. Gresham (Lyon County); and W.F. Cherry (Carlisle County). The following day the paper reported that the jury was deadlocked after seven hours. Gresham and Cherry were for acquittal; the rest found for Robert Hollowell. Judge Evans dismissed the jury.

A new trial began in May for the Night Riders. To ensure that the jury would not be compromised again, a panel from Jefferson and Bullitt Counties, 200 miles away, heard the case. The jury got the case late on May 13 and rendered their verdict on May 14. The Night Riders were fined $35,000 in damages. The Night Rider movement withered and died. For a time, a common reply of a farmer in Caldwell County to the query, "What are you doing?" was "Plowing corn for Mary Lou."

9. World War and Depression

Before the conflict was over, the government mobilized everything during the First World War—even human thought. The nation marshaled men, resources, and later, even opinions. Early on, the raids by Francisco "Pancho" Villa across the Mexican border into the United States attracted more space in the local newspapers than did the bloodshed at the Marne and elsewhere in Europe. After 1916, more attention was given the worsening situation in Europe. It was a relief to read that President Woodrow Wilson ran again on a platform affirming "Peace, Prosperity, and Preparedness." Still, the incumbent Wilson barely squeaked by challenger Charles Evans Hughes in the presidential election. There was a consensus that sacrifice for one's country was honorable and that costs were to be expected. Still, it paid to be cautious.

The resumption of unrestricted submarine warfare on January 31, 1917, by Germany was a calculated risk to knock the United Kingdom out of the war before the United States could have an effect. While food did reach critical levels in England, Germany's plan did not anticipate the speed with which the United States could mobilize, move troops to Europe, and contribute to the battle line in France. The United States turned a professional army of 130,000 into more than 3.5 million in record time. Individuals rushed to volunteer their services to the armed forces, and men that did not faced the draft. "Work or fight" was a popular slogan for men between 18 and 45.

One poignant example of patriotism in Paducah was the enlistment of Conroy Dorian in the Navy. While in training at Great Lakes, Michigan, Conroy caught influenza and died. Eight days later, his brother Charles Dorian replaced Conroy in his nation's service. More than 2,500 Paducahans participated in the war, including William Stuart Nelson, a young black man who not only was commissioned as an officer, but also led troops in combat with the 367th Infantry, 92nd Division. In the rigidly segregated army of the time, this was a remarkable accomplishment. Stuart was the son of Dr. W.H. and Emma Nelson. Later, he became head of several major universities and had a park named for him in Paducah.

Not all who went to France were men. Miss Mary Wheeler served in the Red Cross, where she used her musical skills to entertain the troops. Later, she earned a master's degree, taught at Paducah Junior College, and collected folk songs, including river work songs. (In World War II, she returned to work with the Red Cross.)

LEFT: *This young black Paducahan, William Stuart Nelson, led troops in combat during World War I, a rare occurrence due to the racism of the period.*
RIGHT: *Mary Wheeler went to France with the Red Cross in 1918, and served with them again during World War II. (Courtesy MHM.)*

A veteran called back into active duty was the gunboat USS *Paducah*. Anna May Yeiser, daughter of Paducah's mayor, christened this vessel on October 11, 1904, in New Orleans. Despite the fact that its design and purpose was to operate in shallow waters, the craft served off Gibraltar and was credited with a successful attack on a submarine.

One byproduct of the war was a decline in streetcar passengers, which led to the demise of the streetcar line in Paducah. The line, operated by Stone Webster of Boston, went into receivership early in September 1918 despite heroic efforts by the firm. A new brick car barn on West Broadway and double tracking of Broadway between Fourth and Seventeenth was too little, too late. The line had petitioned the City to raise the rates from 5¢ to 7¢ per fare. Still, deficits grew and the firm went bankrupt.

Another way Paducahans contributed to the war effort was to observe certain days as special days of abstinence. The day September 15, 1918, was declared to be "gasoline less" by Charles Wheeler, fuel administrator. The chief of police, Henry Bailey, promised that any driver ignoring the order in the city would be arrested, either by the police or by uniformed "Home Guards."

Liberty Bond rallies gave citizens of Paducah the chance to donate directly to the war effort. On September 19, 1918, 12 floats "lighted by electricity" came from St. Louis at the request of the chairman of the bond drive, George

The PG-18 USS Paducah *was christened by Anna May Yeiser on October 11, 1904. (Courtesy MHM.)*

Goodman. A grand parade entertained the community. The people gaped in amazement at the wonders of electricity on the move and responded generously to the cause. The quota for McCracken County was $1,406,000. Two days after this quota was announced, Temple Israel pledged one-fourteenth of the total, $100,000, giving the other churches and civic organizations in the community a goal to match.

Despite the furor associated with the war effort, there still was much of "business as usual" in Paducah in 1918. A lack of dog muzzles in the local stores caused comment in the newspapers as it took the teeth out of the recent ordinance requiring all such animals to be restrained in public. Both the Robinson's and the Ringling Brothers Circuses performed in Paducah in 1918. Robinson's 22 tents attracted a large crowd on September 8. The performances marked the 94th annual tour of the company. The Ringling Brothers show was not as fortunate. On September 20, soggy ground delayed the performance. Nevertheless, the crowds that came expecting to see the circus took the opportunity to engage in heavy trading in local shops.

October 1918 proved most trying for Paducah and the nation. Spanish influenza swept across the country, not respecting age, sex, religion, or political party. In all, there were 2,008 cases of flu and 166 cases of pneumonia in Paducah and its environs.

Twenty-four deaths were attributed to the disease. Drastic measures in the city included closing of public houses, schools, churches, and the banning of all public meetings. Those forced to meet the public in their daily work routine felt like soldiers at the front. Restrictions were lifted on the same day that the German Kaiser announced his abdication and fled to the Netherlands. The "Great War" was over. The country was ready to celebrate.

Women voted for the first time in municipal elections in 1919. One issue was whether or not to support the sale of bonds to finance the construction of a new high school. The sons of Confederate General Lloyd Tilghman, Frederick and Slidell, had been on the last boat up the Tennessee to Confederate lines when Kentucky declared for the Union in 1861. Both were successful on Wall Street and made their hometown an offer. They would purchase property for a new high school if the City would name it for their mother, Augusta. Voter registration proved to be the largest ever with 2,657 signed for the Democrats and 2,283 Republicans. Of this number, 2,291 (46 percent) were women.

In the fall of 1922, labor violence associated with the nationwide railroad strike spilled over into Paducah. Homes were fired on. Three bombs exploded in the city on September 1. One was detonated at 229 Harahan, the home of the master mechanic of the Illinois Central Railroad shops, Joseph F. Walker. Another went off at 1900 Trimble at S.E. Stanley's house. Stanley also worked on car repairs for the railroad. The third bomb damaged the house of Mrs. O.M. Fields at 1326 Langstaff Avenue, perhaps as a warning to the brother of Mrs. Fields, also employed by the Illinois Central. Headlines in the local newspapers blamed the bombings on "reds" rushing through the streets of Paducah hurling dynamite bombs from the windows of speeding automobiles and called for action. Like other parts of the world, a growing fear associated with the recent success of socialist parties in Mexico and Russia began to permeate the national psyche in the United States. This tended to exacerbate another trend that also was growing—xenophobia, or the fear of foreigners, which led to de facto exclusion of immigrants in the 1920s.

The day following the bombing of Mrs. Fields, Stanley and his neighbor James Drew, whose house had been fired on earlier, saw two men in the neighborhood acting suspiciously. The men ran, and the two fired six shots at them as they

A circus parade in 1918 enlivened a community recently inured to sacrifice for the war effort. (Courtesy JJ.)

chased the pair through Oak Grove Cemetery. No harm was done, but the City did impose a curfew.

The U.S. marshal for Western Kentucky, Thomas Needham Hazelip, dispatched two deputies from Louisville to assist local law enforcement efforts to apprehend the bombers. Two men were arrested, but the federal district court released one. The other served six days in the county jail for disregarding a court injunction.

While concerned over the labor violence, Paducahans were optimistic that national efforts would resolve the railroad problems. There was a local issue that attracted considerable attention. A petition circulated suggesting that the commission form of government was not needed. More than 3,000 signed the document and the matter was put on the ballot in November. The *News-Democrat* tried to sway the election by supporting the existing form; however, the voters, by three to one, elected to return to the aldermanic-council form of government in one of the lightest votes in the history of the city. Only Scott precinct, containing the residences near Seventh and Broadway, favored retaining the commission form. Partisan politics returned to local elections.

In 1923, the city prepared to elect a new administration. The Ku Klux Klan made an effort to gain recognition in Paducah before the election. A national organizer, Dr. E.H. Lougher, announced his plan to speak at the tobacco warehouse at Tenth and Broadway. Dr. J.R. Crawford, pastor of the Kentucky Avenue Presbyterian Church, assailed the hooded knights and denounced the "whole pesky band" who took it upon themselves to be the conscience of "100% Americans." Mayor pro tem L.A. Washington and Commissioner Wynn Tully

Central Fire Station, seen here 1906, shows an era when horses ceased to reign and internal combustion engines came into acceptance as reliable means of delivering fire service. (JJ.)

Prior to World War I, life had been pleasant for many young adults in Paducah. Here, Dorothy Billington and her friends pose for the camera in 1913. (Courtesy the Blalock and Stacey families.)

joined with Claude C. Pace, commissioner of public safety, in opposition to the Klan rally. The city officials sent 18 police officers to watch the Klan and prevent any violence. A hostile crowd gathered, numbering between 350 and 500. Some came out of curiosity and some crossed over the street after leaving the nearby Elk's circus at the end of its performance to see what was happening. Finally, the Klansman gave up trying to speak.

Women were candidates in both parties in the city elections. Mrs. Joe F. Post ran for alderman on the Democratic ticket. Mrs. Francis Allen opposed Republican John J. Dorian successfully for city treasurer. Mrs. Belle Kinsolving vied with Democrat Ross Rutter for city clerk. Generally, the Democrats were successful, carrying the state and the county elections. Dr. J.N. Bailey, with the backing of Hazelip's Republican organization, not only won the office of mayor, but also carried five precincts that traditionally were Democratic. The city of Paducah had Republican mayors for four of the five full terms since 1908. Only during the disputed election of 1916 did the Democrats manage to get control of the office of mayor, and then it took the Court of Appeals, the governor, and a special election.

Democrats carried the city elections in 1924 with the exception of one council seat. Despite this vote, the city gave a plurality to the Republicans in the national contest; however, the county vote put McCracken County into the Democratic camp.

Paducahans learned to regret their hasty decision to return to the mayor-general council form of government. The system was inefficient and cumbersome. Moreover, partisan political issues often clouded local races. Reform was desired again. During the 1926 election, the Democrats won all ten vacancies on the General Council. Voters also opted to return to the commission form of government, but Kentucky law did not permit cities to change their form of organization during the term of city treasurers, clerks, and jailers; therefore, the change could not occur prior to January 1, 1928. There was no doubt about the sentiment of the electorate. The vote for the commission form carried by 2,234 to 466.

Elections in 1927 came at a time of prosperity. Alben Barkley had steered a bill through Congress that promised an opportunity for growth for Paducah and southern Illinois. A contract for $2 million had been awarded to the Paducah, Ohio River Bridge Company (to build the Irvin S. Cobb Bridge connecting Paducah and Brookport). Work began in the fall. Also, the Illinois Central Railroad shops opened. A special edition of the paper commemorated the dedication of the giant plant. A list of local industries at this time confirms the prosperity of Paducah.

Paducah businesses recorded large gains during the previous year. One local newspaper listed new firms in the city on October 20, 1928, on its front page. Preparations were under way for the bridge over the Ohio River. This promised to open the Illinois market to Paducah merchants as never before. The new Cobb Hotel rose on the corner of Sixth and Broadway. Prosperity seemed to favor the Republicans. A record vote turned out to determine the new president. Only 4 of the 34 precincts in Paducah voted for Al Smith, despite his favoring liquor, being a Roman Catholic, and his nomination by the Democratic Party. Herbert Hoover and the Republican Party carried both the city and the state; however, the First Congressional District of Kentucky continued its tradition of voting the straight Democratic ticket.

The Illinois Central Railroad shops and roundhouse were among the largest in the world by 1928. (Courtesy IC/CN Railroad.)

This view shows the opening of the Paducah-Brookport highway bridge on May 8, 1929, linking Western Kentucky with southern Illinois as never before. The route became U.S. 45.

The Depression disrupted life around the world and Paducah was no exception. Like voters in other cities, Paducahans rejected the party associated with this disaster and turned to the Democrats in 1932. One main factor in this transformation here and elsewhere was the realignment of the black vote. The party of Lincoln lost the unquestioning loyalty of African Americans. The primary of 1931 attracted considerable interest and this continued into the general election for offices in Paducah. Ed Scott defeated B.A. Washburn for mayor. Other winners included Charles C. Rieke for finance over Ross Rutter, and Emmet Holt for safety over Wells Heath. George Lock took property over George Hannin while E.R. Bradshaw defeated E.L. Ross for public works. The "outs" continued to replace the "ins."

Paducah changed administrations twice between the crash of the great bull stock market and the awful destruction of the flood of 1937. While not spectacular, these administrations had to deal with the growing problems of unemployment and insecurity that accompanied the Depression. It was during these years that a group of civic-minded Paducahans undertook a remarkable assignment to create a college for the youth of the city so that they could continue their education without leaving home. At a time when one out of every four workers in the nation was on unemployment, Paducah started a private junior college. The creation of Paducah Junior College was an act of faith that defied the miasma of despair prevalent in many communities in 1932. The tuition for the first students was higher than that of the University of Kentucky. Times were hard, but the worst was yet to come.

10. Trials by Water and War

Flooding is a frequent problem for Kentucky since it is served by many rivers that flow north into the Ohio and thence into the Mississippi at Wickliffe. Kentucky's three western counties bordering the Mississippi also suffer from the effects of great floods like that of 1927, which caused $200 million in damage from Cairo, Illinois, to New Orleans.

However, that flood was nothing compared to the devastation of the Ohio Valley during 1937. Four hundred died, 1 million were homeless, and more than $500 million in property was lost throughout the valley, but Paducah, the largest town near the mouth of the Ohio, received the brunt of the damage from the river. Moreover, the Wabash, Cumberland, and Tennessee Rivers added their overage to the swollen Ohio at Paducah.

Over the years, Paducah suffered many disasters, but none equaled the flood of 1937. Much of the business area was damaged by fire in 1852. U.S. Grant seized Paducah in 1861 to prevent its capture by approaching troops from the Confederacy; however, in 1864, Nathan Bedford Forest raided the city twice. Considerable damage was inflicted by the defending troops, who burned blocks of buildings that were used to conceal snipers firing on Fort Anderson, the earthen redoubt constructed in 1861 on the site of the old federal marine hospital to provide shelter for the Federal garrison in Paducah.

Adverse weather proved a more dangerous enemy than invading armies. The first week in February 1902 is remembered as the "White Week." The city was coated in ice. Trees, wires, roofs—nearly everything exposed to the elements—felt the heavy effects of the storm. Damage, estimated at $200,000, was considerable but not devastating. That was not the case in the winter of 1917. Sixteen inches of snow fell on December 8 and more snow followed to a depth of 24 inches by January 13, 1917. The following night, the Ohio River froze to a depth of 8 inches and people walked on the river without fear. Just before dawn on January 29, a great roar announced that the Ohio ice pack was on the move, carrying barges and boats with it. Two days later, the ice on the Tennessee surged down the "chute" formed by Owen Island and the bank, scouring the Paducah riverfront. Damage to river craft reached $1 million. Still, compared to 1937, these events were only minor hindrances to the progress of the city.

Before 1937, floods came frequently in 1815, 1822, 1828, 1832, 1867, 1883, 1884, and 1913. In 1867, the Ohio reached 50.7 feet. That level was surpassed in

The great snow in the winter of 1917 forced Hank Brothers Hardware to pile the excess powder on the curb. (Courtesy Jimmy Hank.)

1884 with a high watermark of 54.2, which was approximately the same level as the flood of 1815. In 1913, floodwaters surpassed the high watermark of 1884, but no major damage resulted. The accepted image of Paducah was that the city was relatively safe from flooding despite the experiences of 1815, 1867, 1884, and 1913. This attitude changed dramatically in 1937, and the fate of the city hung in the balance. Only the construction of a floodwall in the 1940s enabled Paducah to regain its appeal to new businesses.

The Ohio Valley suffered greatly in 1937, but the brunt of that flood was felt in Paducah. The average rainfall for Kentucky was 15.37 inches; for Paducah in the same period, the average was 17.53.

January 1937 opened with rain that continued for two weeks, but Paducahans did not think it ominous. Bobby Marshall, wife of Dr. T.J. Marshall, kept a record of her experiences during the flood. She recalled, "occasionally we would hear someone say that the river was very high, but Paducah had always been high and dry when other cities and towns on the Ohio and Tennessee were flooded, we felt no uneasiness." Instead, citizens of Paducah basked in the success of the city during the past year. City Manager L.V. Bean remarked on January 3, "I think we have just closed a most satisfactory year." Not until January 10 did people begin to take notice of the rising water. (On January 7, the paper noted that Paducah needed to raise matching funds to retain the Work Projects Administration [WPA] projects in the area. In 1936, 500 people worked for the WPA in the Paducah area. At the time, threats of flooding were not noted. The future year looked promising. On January 17, an increase in building was reported.)

The flood in 1884 did little damage but proved to be an omen of things to come. (Courtesy Albert Jones.)

A major problem of the snow in 1917 was where to pile it. Tunnels and clearings had to be cut for pedestrians. (Courtesy MHM.)

The Ohio and Tennessee Rivers froze solid in 1918. (Courtesy MHM.)

An ice and sleet storm paralyzed Paducah on January 10. "We had the worst sleet storm Paducah has ever experienced," wrote Mrs. Marshall. Beautiful shade trees were ruined, she said, and "all telephone, telegraph, and electric light wires were completely wrecked." Kentucky Utilities repairmen were working day and night to recover electricity for the community. People who had stokers that used electricity to feed coal automatically to their furnaces and "who cooked with electricity had to close their homes and go to the hotels or to the homes of friends or relatives in order to keep warm or have food," Marshall wrote. Wires eventually were repaired and everyone felt that the worst was over. Actually, the time of trial was just beginning.

The flood came with surprising speed. Utter isolation compounded the problems generated by the high water. Telephone and telegraph lines were out and even the local radio station went silent. People could only watch the water rise and hope that friends and neighbors were safe. Frank Jones left his job as foreman on the Illinois Central Railroad at 5:00 p.m. on January 19 only to have his car drown out at Twenty-third and Kentucky Streets. A big truck pushed him out, but he had to walk home to Lone Oak, a suburb of Paducah.

City officials realized that extraordinary measures were called for. On January 19, Charles G. Vahlkamp, chairman of the Red Cross, appointed emergency committees. The following day, refugees were housed in the old Southern Hotel at Second and Broadway. Water had closed Jefferson at First Street. The gauge was 51 feet and officials warned that another rise would mean disruption of electric service. The loss of power isolated Paducah. "The thing that made the situation so distressing in Paducah," recalled Marshall, "was that right from the start every means of communication was completely wrecked by that sleet storm, even WPAD radio station, and for three or four days and nights, the outside world knew nothing of our desperate plight."

The market house almost disappeared during the 1937 flood. (Courtesy MHM.)

On Thursday, January 21, people in the downtown area began to talk about the backwater that was creeping into the lower areas of the city. As Mrs. Marshall wrote, "nobody felt that Paducah was in any danger. Certainly we never dreamed that our part of town would be inundated." Dr. Marshall went on a call and by the time he returned, water was about 2 feet deep at Nineteenth and Broadway, two blocks from the Marshall house at 110 Fountain Avenue. The following day brought more sleet and rapidly rising backwater that quickly covered Kentucky, Broadway, Jefferson, and Monroe Streets at Tenth through Thirteenth Streets.

W.L. Beasley Jr. recorded in his diary that he "awoke this morning to find water over a foot deep in the street in front of our house, and we live over a mile from the river." Beasley lived at 1100 South Mallory (Thirteenth Street). Apparently WPAD, the local radio station, went dead on January 23. Beasley noted this event in his diary and remarked that the waters were still rising. He and Charles Houser carried a ton and a half of coal up on the front porch in coal buckets in anticipation of losing use of their furnace in the basement. During the day, "Joe and I pulled up a floor board to rescue a kitten under the house. We fired the furnace until this afternoon when the water poured through the basement window and put the fire out. We then built a fire in the fireplace." The WPAD radio went out and the telephones went dead. Beasley wondered "how the men at the water plant are keeping things going. We are all dog-tired and worn out tonight."

The temperature made a rapid drop that caused many automobile engines to freeze and, before many of these stalled cars could be recovered, the waters closed over them. They remained a hazard to navigation when boats replaced automobiles on the city streets. Waves from passing boats also bounced the hulks about, making their destruction total. Dr. Robert Gordon Matheson, the Dean of

Paducah Junior College, attended a meeting honoring W.C. Johnstone (retiring agricultural agent and father of the present federal judge Edward H. Johnston at Paducah) at the Ritz Hotel at 2201 Broadway on January 23. By the time the meeting ended, water blocked parts of Jefferson near Twelfth Street. The Dean tried to force his car through, only to be drowned out. A passing taxi pushed him through the deepening waters and the car restarted. On arrival at his house, Matheson took the precaution to drive his vehicle up on a pile of ashes so that the motor was raised, thus saving the generator and other vital parts of the motor in the days to follow when the flood covered that area.

Paducahans tried to cope with the rising waters as best as they could. Ray Black lived on Nineteenth Street. He and his son took all of their furniture upstairs and prepared to leave. As they could not take the family cat, they set out food and water for the animal. Conditions were such that they were unable to get back for four days. The waters had destroyed the piano and moved the refrigerator; however, the cat survived. Black remembered that on his return to the house he got a piece of ham out of the refrigerator and put it on a piece of paper to feed the cat. The famished beast ate both the ham and the paper.

Life in Paducah was not easy. On Sunday, January 24, Beasley wrote in his diary, "Our chief concern is keeping well. We are all tired but are carrying on by strength. We are continually bumping into one another and running about through the house. The children are crying and the rest of us are so upset and excited that we are irritable. When someone says something to another, a response may be snapped back at him. We expect the water to be in the house on the first floor by morning."

During an interview in 1981, Mrs. Haleen Wynn, then 74, recalled that her family waited until the waters got into their house before packing a suitcase and fleeing by boat. They put their possessions up as high as possible and left their little dog on a foldout couch with food and water. Both survived but the house was severely damaged by mud. Wynn remembered as the family left, the boat passed under the streetlight at Tenth Street. She said she could have touched the light.

Children viewed the flood in a different light from their parents. James Midyett was a student at McKinley School during the flood and classes closed and were made up at the end of the school term. As the waters rose nearer and nearer the house at 423 Hayes Avenue, sanitation problems arose. The house was cut off from its outdoor toilet. Only James could reach it and then only by the use of stilts.

The population continued to watch the waters rise. W.L. Beasley recorded on Monday, January 25, that "it gives us a feeling of utter helplessness, for there is nothing one can do to keep it out or stop it. The water is rising now about an inch every two hours." Still, hope springs eternal. "The sun came out, which makes us all feel better." Beasley heard over the restored WPAD that the Red Cross was planning to move the population to the camps established in the west end with the aid of the Coast Guard and the Tennessee Valley Authority (TVA). He also noted that the city water was to be cut off and they were advised to fill every available container to last until they could be rescued.

Weather reports on January 26 promised no relief. Beasley wrote that he heard "that the river will rise several more feet and the water is two feet deep downstairs now, so the folks are alarmed and we have decided to leave at once." Throughout the city people had to decide when to leave and what could be taken with them. Even the hospitals had to move. Mrs. Marshall reported that Riverside Hospital was evacuated first, then the hotels. The Illinois Central Hospital (located at 1423 Broadway) was the last to be moved. The dead were moved to second floors of the different funeral homes until they could be evacuated.

In 1981, Mrs. Lovie Fields recalled that they lived on Twelfth and Jones Streets during the flood and were taken by barge to Twenty-eighth, where Boy Scouts helped them off the barge. She was put on a truck and taken to Mayfield to wait out the waters. On the way, she noted pianos, clothing, and other goods floating on the filthy water. Dogs, cats, and even rats would all be marooned together on tops of houses and not fighting. Beasley commented on a similar event he witnessed. He and his brother fed five cats and a dog on the roof of their garage. The animals had been rescued from various houses "and they seem so thankful to be here that they get along with each other just fine."

Frank Carlson left his house at Fifteenth and Broadway in a boat he built himself. He too went to Mayfield and the family moved to Mississippi to stay with relatives. As he was leaving, he noted a cow on the second-floor porch of a house in the downtown area. The cow survived and received national attention when a photographer from *National Geographic* captured her image.

Paducah attracted national attention when National Geographic *ran a photograph of this "cow loft." (Courtesy MHM.)*

The flood hit members of the African-American community hard. Tim Jones interviewed Dorothy Titsworth in 1981 as a class project for Dove Anna McNabb Elementary School. She recalled that her family lived at 1314 Rudy Avenue and the water was at the back door before they decided to leave. First, they went to West Kentucky Vocational School, where the Red Cross provided food. Most slept on the floor, but her family had managed to salvage their bedding. She vividly remembered how difficult the living conditions were. One woman brought a rooster and a pig and insisted on keeping them with her until complaints mounted and she was forced to throw them into the waters. Noble Clark remembered going into his brother's house with Ed Wade and finding two dogs floating on a daybed. The animals were rescued.

Lack of food distressed many of those trying to wait out the flood, particularly in the black community. Oscar Cross remembered that the police told those housed at Lincoln High School to get any food they could from the submerged stores. The refugees made johnboats and broke into the Roof Brothers grocery. Benjamin F. Blakely reported that his group "got our food from the N.C. Freight house. We got out milk from the Goldbloom. We got our clothes from different stores and we went to a tobacco barn to stay." The N.C. Freight was the Nashville, Chattanooga & St. Louis Railroad Company and the Goldbloom was a local dairy. Many of the boats used were characterized as "johnboats" at the time. These were shallow draft, ungainly craft that lacked centerboards, making them difficult to steer in rapid waters. A classic example of the too frequent result of relying on such craft was the experience of Frank Walter Rein of Paducah, who was marooned for a time at the Illinois Central Shops at Fifteenth and Kentucky Avenue. "Saturday [January 23] we got some lumber from the carpenter shop and built a johnboat. Two of the men, Ardie Bell and another man, pushed it over to a wholesale grocery house—I believe it was M. Livingston at 11th and Kentucky Avenue." They filled the boat but it capsized on the return trip and they lost all their supplies.

The flood challenged traditional social conventions as time passed. In one instance recalled by O.K. Vick, two young, single refugees had to share the same room. Each worked different hours; therefore, they did not meet. Nevertheless, the young lady did find it embarrassing to admit that she shared her bed with a young man.

Vick was a Boy Scout at the time and played a role of some importance during the flood. On one occasion, Vick recalled that his troop went back into the downtown area, broke a window on the second floor of the Cobb Hotel, and gathered up the blankets there to provide for the refugees lodged in the Lone Oak High School. According to Vick, a local meat packer agreed to donate food for the refugees at Lone Oak if someone would pick it up. Vick and other scouts, aged 14 to 15, walked from the school to the plant and back with about 50 pounds of meat per person. The round trip was approximately 6 miles. One of the last refugees to leave Paducah was Mary Margaret Hoffman. In an interview with the author on February 6, 1980, she recalled that her family saw a sign at the Mayfield city limits that said, "Refugees, Don't Stop Here." It was not that the people were lacking in compassion. Rather, they were full. The Hoffmans went to Wickliffe.

Lack of communications created many hardships during the flood. Family members were separated and unable to learn the fate of others for long periods. False rumors circulated. The entry of Beasley in his diary for January 27 said that "WPAD said that an order had just come through from Washington for everyone to leave Paducah immediately and we were about to get in our boat when WPAD said it was all a mistake and a city official assured us there was nothing to fear, that the river would not rise much more and it would be better if those comfortably situated would stay where they were and not be an extra burden on the Red Cross." Relieved, he and his brother unpacked.

The *Paducah Sun-Democrat* for January 30 was published as complete evacuation of the town was under the supervision of the military. Captain Glen Peterson had been in Paducah with the Civilian Conservation Corps camp, and he welcomed the arrival of regular troops from Fort Sheridan, Illinois, to augment the personnel he had at Paducah. Companies B and C of the 2nd U.S. Infantry were led by Captains William H. Collette and Walter Winn of the regular army. The soldiers supervised the evacuation of the city. In a ten-day period, 22,000 registered as refugees at Arcadia School on the west side of the city. From there, the refugees fanned out, looking for sanctuary.

Beasley's diary for January 30 reported, "It is now about 59 feet deep. A passer-by has just told us that 150 troops will be here tomorrow to force everyone to evacuate in the interest of health. This afternoon, Dad, who had gone out with the rest of the family, paddled up in a boat and we were certainly glad to see him. He reported that they had all gotten out safely and were staying in Mayfield. He said it was true about the soldiers and that he had come to get us and some clothes for the family." Beasley and his older brother, Joe, left the next day, rowed 2 miles to dry land, and caught a ride to Mayfield, where he rejoined his family.

The threat of epidemic caused health officials throughout the Ohio Valley to insist on mass inoculation against typhoid. Fifty years later, the resulting sore arms are still remembered by survivors of the flood. No major outbreak occurred despite the overcrowded conditions in many of the refugee camps.

The crest had been at 60.8 feet on February 2. On the same day, 12 men were arrested for looting. Since the jail was under water, the offenders were housed in a secure building at the rear of the Jack Keiler home at 3010 Broadway until they could be transported to Mayfield to await trial. The following day, another shock hit the city. The loss of electric power had forced the closing of the city water plant; therefore, the fire mains had no pressure. A fire started in a grain elevator on the south side of Madison between Tenth and Eleventh Streets and spread to nearby houses. Firemen watched helplessly as the structures entrusted to them burned to the water line. A night patrol helped prevent further looting and the army set up patrols and required passes of all entering the flooded area.

All was not gloom and doom for refugees. Children from the Friendly Home, along with Miss Vonie Young and Mrs. Phoebe McGee, were having a grand

The flood gave a submerged "No left turn" sign in Paducah's business district a new meaning in 1937. (Perhaps one could turn to the "port" side.) (Courtesy MHM.)

time. These orphans were housed in the Country Club and had a golf course for a recreational area.

"River's Long Reign at End" was the headline of the *Paducah Sun-Democrat* on February 18. Over seven-eighths of the city had been under water for a month and 22,000 refugees fled to shelters in Kentucky and Tennessee. Silt, slime, and muck greeted the refugees and had to be removed. All basic services—lights, water, gas, and sanitary sewers—had to be renovated. Buildings had to be inspected to see if any structural damage had resulted. An inspection committee consisting of members of the fire department and representatives of local architects arranged to issue permits for return to flooded structures. In particular, boilers had to be inspected to prevent their exploding. The Citizens Bank had a peculiar problem. Items in the vaults had to be retrieved. A commercial drier used by dry cleaners (called a mangle) was purchased and women were employed to operate it so that customers could dry their valuable documents. Before calling the customer in, the safety deposit boxes were tilted and surplus water allowed to drain out. Upon arrival of the customer, the boxes would be opened with the customer having the option of cleaning the contents themselves or take advantage of the help provided by Citizens Bank. One of the largest depositors in the banks insisted that one particular bank employee assist. Needless to say, the bank complied. Damage at Paducah was estimated at $27,610,000, including $6.43 million in losses to businesses. Plate glass replacement alone cost $125,000.

A Coast Guard cutter made use of Broadway in 1937. (Courtesy McCPL.)

Even before the waters dropped below the 56-foot mark, a committee looked forward to the rebuilding of Paducah. City Manager L.V. Bean met with city leaders including Con W. Craig, Harry Meyer, Max Miller, and George Runge and set goals for repopulating the town. Harry Hopkins of the WPA, A.B. "Happy" Chandler, governor of Kentucky, and other officials of state and federal governments came to see the extent of the damage and went away impressed at the devastation. They joined with Senator Alben Barkley of Paducah in urging Congress to pass a federal program to provide low-cost interest loans to assist in rebuilding the ravaged towns along the Ohio River. On February 13, Tom Waller, a local attorney, went to Washington to represent Paducah at a conference of mayors with Hopkins. Waller urged the consolidation of relief efforts through one agency to ease the red tape. Eventually, 51 different agencies pooled their resources in behalf of the flood-stricken cities. Roy Wilkins of the NAACP visited the Ohio Valley and was surprised at the lack of racial discrimination in Louisville; in Paducah, two black doctors, G.A. Davis and P.M. Fernandez, worked day and night and the Red Cross made no provision for food and shelter other than refugee tickets.

As the waters receded, bodies appeared. On February 14, the body of Uel Park, 23, of 1315 Langstaff Avenue was recovered. He had fallen out of a boat and drowned. Park's father survived the accident by clinging to a utility pole until rescuers reached him. Two days later, William and Stella Alcock, both over 65, were found in their three-room house on Pool Road lying in the kitchen. Tom Wall of 1317 Monroe was found in his bed wrapped in blankets and was believed to have died before the flood. Jim Beach of 621 Park Avenue was also found in bed, apparently the victim of a heart attack. James Stokes, 61, of 635 Flournoy also was recovered wrapped in his bed clothing. None but Parks was directly related to drowning, but the cold, worry, and exertion took its toll on the ill and aging. The final victims were not discovered until March 24, when the bodies of Mrs. Emma Skillian and her older sister, Lizzie Petter, were found on the bed of their "gun-barrel" house at 1015 Washington Street. The water reached within 18 inches of the ceiling of the structure and the aged sisters were unable to escape and drowned. The intense cold had delayed the discovery of the bodies for more than two months.

The newspaper for March 7 carried a special section on the flood and its impact on Paducah. Pictures revealed the extent of the damage throughout the Ohio Valley. An article by Edwin B. Greenwald summed up the sense of isolation that Paducah experienced during the first few days of the flood when the city was cut off from the rest of the commonwealth and without the resources to deal with their plight. For the first time many Paducahans realized how pervasive the devastation had been.

One of the first concerns of Paducahans was to avoid the reoccurrence of such floods. On February 19, a town meeting was held to discuss the possible construction of a "seawall" around the city. Two days later a mass meeting was

Prior to 1913, floods, such as this one in February 1897, were an occasion for demonstrating creative navigation on the 1200 block of South Sixth Street. The backwater caused little damage, but all this changed dramatically in 1937. (Courtesy JSJ.)

held to air the topic and a petition was sent to Congress on February 22. Estimated cost of the levee was $5.3 million and the Rotary Club and the Workers Alliance endorsed the project.

Prior to the flood, entertainment in Paducah centered in the home, often around the piano. WPA cleanup workers found more than 2,500 of the estimated 3,200 pianos in the city ruined by the flood. As a piano was heavy and awkward to move quickly, most were placed on raised platforms and left. On their return, many Paducahans were surprised to see their prized pianos still intact. However, with one touch, the instruments often collapsed since the glue had dissolved. The remains of the pianos were hauled to a gully near the Illinois Central roundhouse. Afterward, Paducahans adopted the radio, becoming consumers of entertainment.

The damage to Paducah from the 1937 flood exceeded that of any other major city in the commonwealth. The entire city was evacuated during the worst of the winter at the insistence of both local and federal officials. Also, the absence of fire protection due to the loss of pressure in the city water mains led to several uncontrolled fires causing severe property damage. Perhaps the most serious damage to the city was the change in perception of the site. No longer would Paducah be considered safe from its rivers. This new attitude deterred prospective businesses from choosing Paducah until the floodwall was completed shortly after the end of World War II. Shortages during the war delayed the manufacture of the steel gates needed to complete the floodwall; however, construction on the levee embankments continued. War demands also delayed the production of the massive pumps needed even if the wall and gates were in place. Without these, a major flood could break into the city via the sewers.

The U.S. Army Corps of Engineers conducted an extensive worst-case flood assessment of the Paducah area in 1968 at the request of the Paducah-McCracken

Work on the floodwall started immediately after the 1937 flood. The war years delayed installation of the steel gates. Note the absence of heavy equipment. (Courtesy JJ.)

After the completion of the floodwall, Paducah felt safe once again from the Ohio floods. (JJ.)

County Planning Commission. It determined that with the present system of flood control available from the dams on the Ohio at Smithland, on the Tennessee at Kentucky Dam, and on the Cumberland at Barkley Dam and the floodwall at Paducah would prevent a recurrence of the damage from a flood like that of 1937.

Few at this time paid any attention to the civil war in Spain, and when Europe went to war in 1939, Paducahans were interested but not alarmed. The *Paducah Sun-Democrat* for January 10 used as filler the story of patrolman Reed Kennedy killing pigeons at Sixth and Kentucky.

The next month, fears of another flood occupied Paducah; however, the crest this time was only 42 feet. Still, the town kept up agitation for a floodwall and construction began on April 3. Hitler's move against the Czechs that spring did not cause undue alarm. Europe seemed far removed and other things caught the headlines. The World's Fair opened in New York in May and the youthful king and queen of Great Britain visited the United States in June, capturing the hearts of many in the former colonies. In Paducah, the new Coca-Cola bottling plant opened and promised jobs. The future looked bright.

Despite the gains women had made since World War I, men continued to dominate the labor force in downtown Paducah. One example was Citizens Bank. Men were expected to wear coats, regardless of the weather, during banking hours. Once the doors closed in summer though, off came the jackets, and the porter, Bane Barton, went across the street to Heinie and Tyler's for some of their famous Limburger sandwiches for the staff or to Orr's Chili Parlor. Then, they worked to balance, regardless of how long it took.

The male domination at the bank began to wane with the onset of the draft. Charles Hill was one of the first to be inducted and went to camp in Louisiana.

He was not to be the last. The row of stars the bank kept to acclaim its men in the armed forces reached seven. Gradually, women had to be hired to replace the departed men. The war had an effect on the dress code as well. Women were expected to wear hose, even when they became scarce. One former employee recalls that the president C. Morton Hand may have suspected that some of the women were using pancake makeup on their legs instead of the departed silk or the unavailable nylon (the trick was to center a dark line on the back of the leg that looked like the seam present in hose at that time); however, he was too much of a gentleman to attempt to confirm his suspicions.

The attack on Pearl Harbor on December 7, 1941, infuriated the average American, and authorities tried to channel that fury and hatred. A rubber and scrap drive in Paducah sent packs of seekers from ages 7 to 70 into every nook and cranny of the community. Many illegal dumps were combed for automobile hulks left over from the flood. Various groups such as scout troops vied to bring in the greatest mass of material. Even the cannon from Confederate General Lloyd Tilghman's Lang Park memorial were donated, along with 1,200 pounds of iron bars from the windows and doors of the Citizens Bank building. Every household was encouraged to save its cooking grease for use in explosives. The local paper proudly showed the massive pile on September 27, 1942.

In the same issue it was reported that the Kentucky Ordnance Works was under construction. This plant, located west of Paducah, employed hundreds from the area in the manufacture of TNT. The paper also noted that work was plentiful in and around Paducah. With the increased need for workers in defense projects, the hard times of the Great Depression were over and economic prosperity seemed imminent. The surrounding communities also saw a rush to the new sites engaged in war production, such as the airplane manufacturing plants and shipyards in Evansville, Indiana.

The war effort took first priority for Americans between 1941 and 1945. Gasoline, tires, even food and clothing were rationed for a time. Gradually sugar,

During World War II, POWs were trucked to Paducah to continue the work on the floodwall. (Courtesy JJ.)

Sacrifice for the war is evident in this view of Citizens Bank at Fourth and Broadway. The iron bars on doors and windows had just been removed for a scrap drive. (Courtesy Robertson's The History of Citizens Bank, 1888–1988.*)*

cigarettes, and candy often went under the counter for favored customers. Black market transactions were abhorred at first, but later gained tacit toleration. The public relied on the radio and the movie theaters to take their minds off the horrors abroad, even if only for a time.

Despite shortages of steel and other vital materials dedicated to the war effort, work on the Paducah floodwall continued. In 1944 and 1945, prisoners of war were shipped to the city to help on the project during a threatened flood. As no steel gates were available, the openings in the wall had to be plugged with sandbags.

Nearly 5,000 men and women from the Paducah area served in the military during World War II, according to the May 8, 1945 *Paducah Sun-Democrat.* Many of Paducah's young men rushed to join the military, and others were in the group from the ages of 20 to 44 who were eligible for the draft (the range had been 21 to 35 before Pearl Harbor). Some earned distinction, like Gus Ed Hank III of the family that ran the hardware store on Broadway. Hank earned a Silver Star, Bronze Star, and a Purple Heart during bitterly hard fighting while leading an infantry unit of the 78th Division fighting in the Hurtgen Forest and in the Battle of the Bulge in Germany.

Eugene Paro, later an admiral, commanded a submarine in action in and around the Phillipines. Paducah's own 715 Railway Operating Battalion kept Ed Hough, Johnny Katterjohn, David Carlson, Herman Fields, Bobby Johnson, J.T. Poyner, and others together throughout the war. These Paducah men and others formed fast friendships that have endured long after the war. Under Captain Robert Kelly, this outfit served in North Africa and later in Italy, fighting an enemy that was usually heavily entrenched and determined to hold their positions or extract maximum losses from their foes.

Ray Elliot landed at Guadalcanal and participated in most of the major battles in the South Pacific while serving in the U.S. Marine Corps. Augusta Tilghman High School football hero Jessie Tunstill joined the Air Corps only to be shot down. He later said he appreciated his previous physical training, as it helped him survive German prison camp. Fellow Paducahan Lane Peck, the co-pilot of a B-17, was shot down earlier and arrived in the same camp prior to Tunstill. While walking across the parade ground one day, Peck bumped shoulders with another American and realized it was Charles Broach from Reidland. The two graduates of Reidland High School enjoyed a brief reunion before Broach was moved to another camp. However, it wasn't long before Peck and Tunstill met Frank Young of Paducah, who had also been shot down in a B-17. Peck and Young graduated together from Paducah Junior College in 1940.

For most servicemen and women in World War II though, the opportunity to serve with people from one's hometown was relatively rare. A sense of estrangement and isolation was a common experience. Many weren't even that fortunate, like one lad of 18 who graduated from Augusta Tilghman High School; he was inducted, sent to France as a replacement after the Normandy landing, and killed on his first day in combat. Families of servicemen and women displayed flags in their windows that had a blue star on a white field with a red border. When this was replaced with a gold star, it marked a tragedy for both the family and the entire nation. For those who made it, homecoming was warm and appreciation enduring.

The Second World War made Paducahans dependent on movies, both for news and entertainment, as well as for fund-raising for the war effort. (Courtesy MHM.)

11. The Shift from Steam to Atom

The New Orleans & Ohio Railroad suffered from raids by Nathan Bedford Forrest and by irregulars during the Civil War; however, the Union commander kept the railroad repaired since it was a vital communications link. At the end of the Civil War, the railroad faced financial difficulties. Judge Flournoy succeeded Judge James Campbell as president of the line in 1865. Despite the efforts of these able men, the company continued to suffer financial decline until February 1869, when the railroad was sold at auction to the highest bidder. Eckstein Norton purchased the line, which went through reorganization and became the Paducah & Gulf Railroad Company on February 26, 1869. Two other lines were added on January 31, 1872, with Norton still president. Nevertheless, the company could not survive the Panic of 1873. In March 1878, a new organization known as the Memphis, Paducah & Northern emerged to take over the route. In 1881, Collis P. Huntington purchased both the Paducah & Memphis and the Paducah & Elizabethtown Railroads and formed them into the Chesapeake, Ohio & Southwestern (CO&SW) system with a direct connection between Louisville and Memphis via Paducah.

The General Assembly of Kentucky authorized the Paducah & Elizabethtown Railroad on March 5, 1867. Construction began in 1869 and the railroad opened on September 6, 1872. For the first time, the Purchase region of Kentucky had a direct, all-weather connection with Louisville and Memphis, with a blacksmith's shop, boiler shop, and brass foundry. The initial investment in these units was estimated at $107,000.

The financial panic of 1893 forced Huntington to sell a part of his holdings, including the Chesapeake, Ohio & Southwestern. The Illinois Central acquired ownership of the system in December 1893; however, a series of lawsuits prevented the transfer of the title until August 1896. This section was then known as the Kentucky Division.

The other trunk line entering Paducah was built with the City's support. In the council meeting on January 28, 1889, an agreement allowed the City to purchase $100,000 of bonds to aid in the construction of the Paducah, Tennessee & Alabama Railroad. Work began immediately. Eventually, this line became a part of the Nashville, Chattanooga & St. Louis Railway; and, since the Second World War, a part of the Louisville & Nashville system. The line ran from Paducah to Bruceton, Tennessee, via Benton, Murray, and Paris but now has been abandoned.

Immediately following the Civil War, Lawrence S. Trimble of Paducah organized the Paducah & Illinois Bridge Company to span the Ohio River. The membership included John A. Logan and Ambrose E. Burnside, former generals in the Federal army, and P.G.T. Beauregard and Absolom M. West, generals in the Confederate service. Failure of the project cost Paducah the principal north-south trunk line between Chicago and New Orleans, as the Illinois Central built such a bridge near Cairo on October 29, 1889. Nonetheless, Paducah remained an important railroad town. Eventually a bridge was built over the Ohio near Paducah.

Paducah spanned the Ohio River with the completion of the Paducah & Illinois (P&I) Railroad Bridge. This company was chartered in Kentucky but actually involved the Chicago, Burlington & Quincey Railroad and the Nashville, Chattanooga & St. Louis lines. Construction continued during World War I. The great ice storm in 1918 destroyed the railroad transfer ferry of the Illinois Central (IC) that handled traffic between Brookport and Paducah with daily runs. Necessity forced the Illinois Central to start using the new bridge of the P&I. This arrangement proved so successful that the Illinois Central built the Edgewood Cutoff line in 1925. This bypass line of 169 miles reduced freight traffic on the main line of the IC and became the route of choice for coal trains from the mines in the Madisonville area to the power plants using fossil fuel in Chicago. These huge trains had 225 hopper cars at 70 tons each, a caboose, and 7 diesel engines (5 in front and 2 coupled in the middle of the train to help pump off the air brakes) using this line on their round trip to Chicago. The location of the TVA Shawnee steam power plant off the P&I added to the importance of this line in the 1950s.

At the turn of the century, the Illinois Central Depot gave many their first view of Paducah. (Courtesy JJ.)

A transfer ferry connected Paducah with Brookport, Illinois, prior to 1918. (Courtesy JJ.)

In 1925–1926, the Illinois Central constructed one of the largest railroad shops in the world at Paducah. This immense plant covered 110 acres, initially cost $11 million, and ranked as the fourth-largest employer in Kentucky. Steam locomotives of the 4-8-2 Mountain class were built at the installation. Twenty were completed in 1942–1943 at a period when the plant was operating at capacity. Still, the workers maintained a remarkable safety record. The shop personnel put in 2,456,776 accident-free man-hours.

Following the Second World War, the shops served as a repair and maintenance point for the Illinois Central and other lines. With the gradual change from steam to diesel, the shops converted to service the new engines. The last steam locomotive refurbished at Paducah between 1957 and 1958 was the 2741. For a time, the shops became the graveyard of steamers. Hundreds of massive steam engines that once pulled up to 99 loads of coal from Dawson Springs southward to Paducah went under the cutting torch. Sleek trains became scrap. Even the giant of the freight service, the 2750, was not spared.

One 2-8-2 Mikado serves as a memorial to the passage of the age of steam. This engine originally was on display at Barkley Park until the City gave Robert Green that site for the construction of the Executive Inn and the Julian Carroll Convention Complex. Now, the engine and several cars rest alongside the floodwall just off Kentucky Avenue to be a part of the railroad museum complex that is in development.

The train shops at Paducah changed ownership but retained their attention to detail. Initially, the plant went to the Paducah & Louisville when Jim Smith and David Reed bought that line from the Illinois Central on August 27, 1986.

The close of WW II was the end of an era in Paducah, as steam locomotives were replaced by diesel electric engines. As the means by which people traveled changed, passenger trains became obsolete, and railroading ceased to be the most important source of employment in Paducah. (JJ.)

The name of the shops changed to VMV to honor three women associated with the owners (the wife and secretary of one partner and the sister of the other) and the shops kept one employee, Charles Marshall (now senior vice president). The work force expanded to ten and the new company began work. Initially, some consideration was given to the possibility of refocusing the plant to include work on large earthmoving equipment and mining equipment, but in 1987 the firm took off after receiving a contract from the Mexican national railroad to remanufacture its diesel electric engines. This work continued to expand and the firm was able to increase its work force. VMV employed about 500, on average, and continues to supply traditional services to an international market.

The original owners sold to a group of investors from Chicago, the Dearborn Partners. Currently, Dimeling, Schrieber and Park of Philadelphia own VMV. The shop at Paducah currently is the largest supplier of parts to the electromotive division of General Motors. VMV kept its heritage, originally touted by the IC, that "Paducah built is quality." The location, the facility, and the dedication of workers make this claim a reality. Yet as the year 2001 drew to a close, the demand for the services of VMV fell again, causing speculation that the plant might close.

During the early days of the Second World War, several new employers appeared in response to the growing demand for greater output from American industry. Kentucky Ordnance Plant began its operations near Paducah. The

Kentucky Dam, located at Gilbertsville on the Tennessee River, was completed in 1944. The presence of these two facilities helped trigger a series of decisions that led to the location of what became a major asset as well as one of the greatest threats to the region—the construction of a gaseous diffusion plant to enrich uranium for the production of atomic weapons and the supporting power suppliers, the TVA Shawnee steam electric generating plant and the similar plant of Electrical Energy Incorporated at Metropolis, Illinois, just across the Ohio River.

Within a short time after the construction of the plant began, the population of the city doubled. Paducah was hard pressed to accommodate the influx. Business boomed and bank clearings in Paducah showed the greatest increase of any community in the nation. Paducah became a national news item. Changes induced during this period still determine part of the character of the community.

"Billion Dollar Atomic Plant for Paducah!" was the headline Paducahans saw on December 14, 1950. The Cold War between the United States and the Soviet Union and its allies, especially China, which had only recently turned toward the socialism of Marx, Lenin, and Mao, made it a priority to develop a great supply of more powerful atomic weapons as a deterrent to aggression of the communist bloc against the capitalist nations.

The trigger to this perception was the invasion in 1950 of South Korea by North Korea, with the tacit support of the Soviet bloc. American troops were committed under the auspices of the United Nations by President Harry S. Truman. The Soviet Union was boycotting the U.N. at that time and thus could not veto the action.

The Allied forces just managed to stem the thrust southward at the southern tip of Korea and reinforcements allowed the U.N. forces to push northward, assisted by U.S. Marines who landed above the North Koreans at Inchon. The U.N. forces, under General Douglas McArthur, had air superiority and were able to drive on through North Korea. Late in the year, the combined United Nations forces were in sight of the Yalu River, the boundary between North Korea and China. On November 26, Chinese armies burst from concealment and marched south pushing Allied forces back. The conflict entered a new phase. McArthur asked permission to attack China, with atomic weapons if needed. The perceived need for more and more atomic bombs to stem the human tide attacking in endless waves increased the demand for enriched uranium. On November 27, the day after the Chinese crossed the Yalu River, the Atomic Energy Commission (AEC) made the final decision to locate a gaseous diffusion plant at Paducah.

The city experienced shifts in population following the 1937 flood. Areas within Paducah emptied as people sought higher ground in the west end of the city. Avondale Heights, Colonial Heights, Afton Heights, and Arcadia attracted the more affluent. In consequence, there was surplus residential space in the city limits. Soon Paducahans realized that all space would be needed, and more.

The presence of the hydroelectric generating power plant of TVA at Kentucky Dam also influenced the decision of the AEC to pick Paducah for its new plant;

The uranium enrichment plant at Paducah brought jobs, new residents, and 50 years of coverup of radiation hazards to the community maintained in the name of national security. It is the largest employer in the region. (Courtesy Paducah Sun.*)*

however, the dam was not capable of generating sufficient firm power year round to meet the anticipated demands of the new plant. On December 16, 1950, TVA announced plans to build a coal-fired steam generating plant with four units near Paducah. Further, the AEC sought 850,000 kilowatts of steam power to supply the energy needed to produce the enriched uranium, and the projected TVA plant could not supply but half the amount needed. Five private utilities combined to create a new corporation known as Electric Energy Incorporated (EEI), which would supply the remainder. The TVA plant was called the Shawnee Steam Plant and located next to the AEC site. The EEI generators were located at Joppa, Illinois, just across the Ohio River. The estimated number of workers used on these projects ran over 20,000 early in 1951. Paducah began to fill up.

Dr. Ray Mofield of Murray State University observed the boom and noted that housing shortages caused many Paducahans to rent their extra rooms. "Before 1950, a good sleeping room could be rented for $4 or $5 dollars a week," he wrote. "This soon rose to $10 and later, the better locations were getting $15 a week. Finally, in October 1951, the government ordered rent control." Gradually, existing space was taken, yet still more workers arrived. Temporary building met the demand for a time, but eventually the delays in constructing additional housing were resolved and the city then overbuilt. Forest Hills contained 500 units, both single family and apartment. Another 120 family housing units were at Fair Oaks, 76 at California Court, and 70 at the Paducah Apartments. Most of these were completed after the boom passed. Previously, 300 apartments were built at Elmwood Court, 100 units at Anderson Court, and 162 homes in River Oaks subdivision. Black Oaks provided 60 more units.

Much of the floating population was located outside the city and trailer parks sprang up everywhere in the county. "Flattop Village came into being near the plant; later, the nickname changed to Forrestdale. Over 1,500 residents moved in. Dormitory-type buildings at the plant site housed single construction workers," according to Mofield.

Private construction increased to meet the growing demand for housing. Records show that 148 houses were started in 1950. Mofield notes that this was up slightly over the average, perhaps reflecting an increase toward the end of the year after the news of the new plant had been released. "In 1951, the number climbed to 476 and the figure leaped to an astronomical 741 in 1952," he wrote. The peak had passed, but construction continued to be above normal. In 1953, there were 285 starts; in 1954, there were 129; and in 1955, 111. By 1956, there were only 95. Construction within the city put pressure on existing sewers and on the water lines.

The location of the three plants near Paducah had a tremendous effect on the business district of the city. "Shoppers were so thick in the stores it often took an hour just to get the attention of a clerk," Mofield reported. "Many customers walked away in disgust." Another effect of the influx of workers was the upward

As late as the 1950s, vendors of fruits and vegetables set up on Kentucky Avenue and Maiden Alley near the river. Here, Lydia Stone from Kevil takes a noon break from her job at Petter's Supply to shop. (Courtesy JJ.)

pressure on wages for clerks. "Retail stores were harassed by losing many of their experienced clerks too as hundreds flocked to the AEC area to take high paying jobs. Clerks who earned $40 soon found they could make $100 a week or more, and the rush was on," Mofield said.

Lack of personnel reduced the ability of the stores to serve the increasing demand with traditional working hours. "By February 3, 1951, it was evident the stores could not possibly handle the crowds in the number of hours they were operating, so on that date the Retail Merchants Association voted to stay open Wednesday night each week until 8:30 instead of closing at the traditional 5:00 p.m.," according to Mofield. Protest from prayer-meeting people forced the merchants to change from Wednesday to Friday even though it meant working on the Sabbath.

Mofield points out that there was little increase in the actual number of retail establishments in Paducah. Surplus capacity accounts for part of the explanation: "There were no new shoe stores, or ladies' or men's clothing store built during this period." He also reported that one new department store "made its bow" during this period. In fact, "as far as the downtown businesses were concerned, only a few appliance and loan offices were inaugurated." Some expansion did take place out of the downtown area: "Cardinal Point, a million dollar shopping center of eight relatively small stores, was built at 28th and Cairo Road, and many front lawns became used car lots. That was about the extent of the new business as such."

A great number of roadside markets covered every route in and out of the city. Five new drive-in movie theaters were built and four downtown theaters were jammed day and night. Strangely enough, Mofield noted, only one new night club was built in the city although there was only one in town when the boom started. Paducah attracted national attention during this period with its traffic jams. Hordes of people flocked into the downtown area, looking for something to do. Traffic flow became a major headache for the city.

This view shows Broadway toward the river from the ten-story bank building on Fourth.

This view away from the river shows Broadway from the ten-story bank building on Fourth.

Mayor Robert Cherry faced problems much like that of mayors Sauner and Fisher during the Civil War. Paducah was overflowing with outsiders, and the boomers were not restricted this time by military discipline. Criminals might try to exploit the relative weakness of the Paducah police force, but first, something had to be done to handle the increased traffic. A separate traffic department was established with a captain, a lieutenant, a sergeant, and 12 patrol officers out of the total 48 men on the force. Thirteen new officers were employed and an auxiliary force was organized to help with traffic flow.

Mayor Cherry also increased the budget for the police from $168,693 for 1951 to $199,648.11 in 1952 (why the 11¢ is unknown). Additional increases were made in 1953 to a total of $245,928.42. As a result, there were no insurmountable traffic problems. Cherry helped reduce the traffic congestion by diverting the flow. Both Broadway and Jefferson were made one-way streets from the river to Seventeenth Street to alleviate the bottleneck in the downtown area. Crime rose in the city, but dropped noticeably after 1954, as can be seen in the following figures:

	1953	1954
Arrests	7,379	3,822
Murders	8	0
Assaults	103	27
Sex Offenses	18	9
Common Drunkenness	3,494	2,279
Disorderly Conduct	577	231
Drunken Driving	326	181
Speeding	764	141
Running Stop Signs	645	137
Accidents	1,534	796
Injuries	252	104

The Illinois Central Railroad built this hospital in Paducah to serve its growing work force. (JJ.)

The influx of people put a serious strain on hospital space in Paducah. Riverside and the Illinois Central hospitals were near capacity without the additional load. The Baptists rushed to construct a new facility starting in 1951 and opening in late 1953. Built in 1905, Riverside was a municipal hospital. In July 1959, the City transferred ownership to the Roman Catholic Diocese of Owensboro. The Sisters of St. Francis of Tiffin, Ohio, assumed the operation at Paducah on September 19, 1959, and changed the name to Lourdes. A new facility on Lone Oak Road opened in 1973. From this beginning, Paducah has developed into a regional medical center.

Next to housing and hospital beds, the greatest shortage produced by the boom was in accommodations for schoolchildren. Fortunately, Paducah was prepared. Dr. Mark Scully, the superintendent of schools, had just written a dissertation on how to expand the Paducah school system. Enrollment in 1950 was 4,930, but by early 1951, an additional 300 students had to be handled. In 1952, the city schools had to provide for 5,747 children without any additional funding (no government funding was available to assist the school system until 1953). The highest point in the enrollment cycle was reached in 1953 with 6,337 students, and the year 1954 only had a reduction of 3 students.

The only way to raise the money needed to build new schools was by putting the bond issue on the ballot in a general election. "The city began building its new high school plant, but it was not completed until 1955, and formal dedication of the new $3,000,000 building did not come until June 3, 1956," Mofield said. All money for the project came from local sources. "When federal funds were finally given in 1953, they were used to build a new addition to Brazelton Junior High . . . including eight classrooms, a cafeteria, and auditorium-gymnasium; Clark school got . . . eight classrooms, a cafeteria and kitchen; Jackson . . . built five new classrooms, a kitchen, and a heating plant." In addition, federal funds provided two-thirds of the money for Northside, which replaced three outmoded schools. Forest Hills School was built entirely with federal funds. Local monies also improved Morgan, McKinley, Jefferson, and Lincoln High Schools.

Churches in the city found themselves in an enviable position. They, like so many other institutions, were at the point of saturation. It was not uncommon to have two or three services to meet the demand. Many expanded their physical plant; however, as the suburbs grew, construction began on facilities outside the city limits. With time there has been a continuing flight of population out of the old city limits in Paducah as in other American cities. Still, many of the churches in the city limits serve members that drive in from considerable distances. The "cake of custom" is hard to break.

Mayor Cherry insisted that the growth of the city must be orderly. The City passed a planning and zoning ordinance in 1918, but this merely identified the business and manufacturing districts at the time. All other property was declared residential. A full-time executive secretary was hired for the planning board (Thomas Burleigh) and the services of a professional planner were secured (Kenneth Shellie Associates of Indianapolis, Indiana). The city commission passed an interim zoning law that served until the master plan was completed about a year later.

Riverside began as a municipal hospital in 1905. In 1959, the City transferred ownership to the Diocese of Owensboro. This building was razed in 2000. (Courtesy MHM.)

The rapid growth of the population in Paducah put increased pressure on the water treatment plant to supply the escalating demand for more water. As a result, a shortage of water developed in the summer of 1951. Mayor Cherry called a halt to non-essential use, such as washing cars and watering lawns. The local system had to be expanded. The city commission gave the water board permission to issue $750,000 in revenue bonds, and $500,000 were issued in April 1952. Immediately, these steps began to ensure the expansion of the water treatment plant that had been built in 1885. The capacity of the system was almost doubled by this local effort.

Sewage treatment also proved to be a problem. Paducah paid for its own treatment plant via a bond issue. The new plant was dedicated on November 3, 1957. Had the City waited, federal help would have been available. In 1956, Congress passed a law to permit payment of one half of the cost of sewage treatment plants required by participants in the Ohio Valley Sanitation Compact.

Paducah managed to meet the challenge of the boom connected with the construction of the AEC plant and the two related steam-generating plants without outside aid. Cherry, like Hazelip in the flood of 1913, exemplified self-reliance. The city even managed to provide recreation sufficient to handle a doubled population. In 1952, Cherry had William Hay of the National Recreation Association survey Paducah. Hay said that the city needed 520 acres of parks for a population of 65,000, but nothing was done due to a lack of funding; however, existing parks were improved with baseball and softball diamonds and additional tennis courts. A full-time recreation director was employed to better utilize the

The staff of the second Illinois Central hospital posed for this c. *1952 portrait. Hallie May Kelly is on the front row, far left. (Courtesy the Hallie May Kelly family.)*

existing parks. The Concert Association could not increase its membership since a 1,850-seat auditorium limited it. Paducahans made do with what was available.

The boom did not bring a great rush of industry to the area as one might expect. Instead, Paducah acquired an image that only now is beginning to diminish. "Labor troubles brought Paducah unwillingly into the national spotlight time and again. The strikes were frequent and exasperating, especially to the Association of Commerce which was trying . . . to sell the Paducah-Calvert City area as the ideal place for new industry to locate." What sold was the image of Paducah as a center of controversy. Articles in *Business Week*, *Time*, *U.S. News and World Report*, *Colliers*, and other national magazines helped perpetuate the image of Paducah as a poor risk for new investment. National attention did not prove beneficial, nor was the image presented justified by the facts.

The number of strikes is disputed because "management and labor would never reveal the number of the various subcontracting firms . . . at Shawnee and Joppa. A list was kept by Bill Powell, city editor of the *Sun-Democrat*, from the strikes that got into print. He came up with a total of 84." Despite the number, the plant was completed ahead of schedule. Furthermore, the project came in under cost estimates.

As the labor-management rift widened, the city administration tried to provide some means of settling most disputes short of a walkout. Mayor Cherry appointed a group that was available to arbitrate disputes. Dr. Robert Gordon Matheson, the Dean of Paducah Junior College, served as chairman. No one on the committee had previous experience in such proceedings, but they were willing and the program proved to be effective. Many potential strikes were avoided. Dean Matheson was selected to serve with the American Arbitration Association as a result of his successful experience in Paducah disputes.

The second half of the twentieth century saw a shift in emphasis in the recruitment of new firms to Paducah. Instead of offering a pool of cheap labor, as had been the case in the 1930s and 1940s, Paducah began to emphasize skilled workers. The advent of a two-year registered nursing program at Paducah Community College was the first such program. Others followed to meet the growing need for skills necessary to a major medical complex in Paducah. Western Baptist and Lourdes Hospitals continue to expand to meet a growing demand for more and better health care.

Two Paducah firms are pioneers in new technology for the twenty-first century. John Williams took an idea that arose in a computer class at the University of Kentucky and applied that technology in the business world with Computer Services Incorporated (CSI). CSI initially served as a clearing point for local banks and expanded into an ever-widening regional organization with diversified applications for a changing work environment.

Research microbiologist Curt Jones began Dippin' Dots in 1988 by freezing ice cream pellets at super-cold temperatures. In 1996 and 1997, *Inc. Magazine* rated the company as one of the top 500 fastest growing in the United States. The product now is offered in several other countries in an expanding market.

12. EDUCATION

Paducah earned an enviable reputation in its public schools in academics, music, and athletics. The rush of the more affluent to the suburbs caused the county system to advance rapidly while the declining tax base in the city put downward pressure on that system beginning in the 1950s. Integration was accomplished without major problems but left many African Americans with the sense of isolation felt by other minorities.

In Paducah, like other parts of the nation, discipline shifted from the iron rule of strong principals such as Walter Jetton at Augusta Tilghman High School to a less confrontational style, which reduced the ability of teachers to control the environment in which they taught. The tragic shooting killing three and wounding several others by a young boy at Heath High School at West Paducah in McCracken County in 1997 illustrates that today's students are vastly different social beings from those who accepted without question the prevailing code of school behavior in an earlier environment. The imposed changes to different modes of teaching put greater emphasis on group learning than on individual accomplishment. Also, the computer came at a time when the bulk of the faculty was of a generation that went through school without any exposure to this new technology.

Tilghman High School maintains a high reputation in athletics, especially in track and field. Declining enrollment after the 1950s moved the school to a lower level of competition. The previous images of old Augusta Tilghman football teams pitted against the likes of Central of Little Rock and Male of Louisville have waned to some degree. Despite its many successes over the years, Tilghman continues to have difficulty on the football field with archrival Mayfield City High School.

Integration caused many in the city to move to the various county schools. As a result, the Paducah city school system has the highest concentration of African-American students in the commonwealth. Blacks constitute about 25 percent of the population within the city of Paducah but consistently account for 50 percent of the students attending the city schools. "White flight" also reduced the funding base in the city.

Private education offers an alternative to public schooling. St. Mary's, organized in 1858 by the Sisters of Charity, is the oldest organized school system in the city of Paducah. Unlike the Dorian School and other private institutions of the past,

A principal at Augusta Tilghman High School, Walter C. Jetton was fondly remembered as a strict disciplinarian and was often called "pussy foot" due to his stealth at creeping up on miscreants in the halls. (Courtesy Paducah City Schools Office.)

St. Mary's thrives. The school now has inter-parochial support and has expanded to offer a pre-K–12 curricula to meet a growing demand. St. Mary's and many of the newer private schools insist upon a religious center to their curriculum. Low student-to-teacher ratios help contribute to their effectiveness and may also explain their popularity. The Community Christian Academy now offers K-12 curricula, as does Victory Christian Academy. An alternative educational approach to either traditional public or private schools is the increasing presence of the home-schooled children. The level of accomplishment of this mode of teaching is difficult to assess until the students enter college or post-secondary training.

Many in Paducah received job skill training at proprietary schools early in the twentieth century. West Kentucky Industrial College offered both vocational and teacher-training classes to African Americans while Lincoln High School focused on a more academic experience. For years, Paducah Central, Draughon's (after 1901), and other "business schools" provided skills for entry into the world of business. New technology replaced shorthand, basic bookkeeping, and typing. Gradually this approach has faded out, beginning with the community college approach that supplied both traditional higher education and business courses.

Paducah Junior College (PJC) came along in 1932 with the goal of a quality two-year liberal arts education. Dr. Robert Gordon Matheson, the "Dean," introduced the concept of the two-year college, responding to the defined needs for technical training in the community by offering courses in "commerce." That combined approach to higher education led to the evolution of Paducah Junior College into a comprehensive community college. PJC merged into the University of Kentucky (UK) system in 1968 as Paducah Community College

"Nat" Dortch taught geology part time at PJC and PCC. A fossil he discovered is named for him.

(PCC) but continued to cooperate with Murray State University (MSU). As a result, it became possible for a student in Paducah to earn a Ph.D. or Ed.D (from UK), various master's degrees (from MSU, UK, and others), bachelor's degrees in many areas, plus three levels of associate's degrees (from PCC and from West Kentucky Technical College) while remaining in Paducah. Paducah Technical College (formerly the Institute of Electronic Technology) was purely technical at first but is moving into a more traditional college curriculum.

Construction of the NASA *Challenger* site at Paducah Community College will add to the opportunities of regional elementary students to see and participate in cutting-edge technology. That, plus the presence of the four-year engineering program of the University of Kentucky located at Paducah Community College near the atomic plant promises further movement toward combining these two entities to develop a national research center for the study of problems stemming from use of atomic energy and the disposal of spent materials.

Despite all the social and economic changes that had to be dealt with while trying to serve the needs of a changing student body and faculty, education in Paducah continues to be equal to or better than all but a few school systems in the commonwealth. Innovative use of technology has emerged and new techniques of teaching have produced positive results. New teachers brought new experience and professional development reinforced the skills of others. Paducah continues to produce national merit scholars and leaders in team sports, music, speech, and theater. Paducah does not have to apologize to anyone for its educational system.

Dr. Robert Gordon Matheson, "the Dean," was a leader in the junior college movement.

Paducah Community College is unusual in that the two-year college also houses a four-year accredited engineering program operated by the University of Kentucky.

13. FUN AND FROLIC

Entertainment in Paducah changed dramatically after the Civil War, when traveling companies began to make regular stops in the new community. In 1860, the brick St. Clair Hall opened at 112–114 South Second Street between Broadway and Kentucky, facing the market. This theater was named for Sallie St. Clair, a popular actress who frequently performed in Paducah.

Following the Civil War, the location of the St. Clair fell out of favor and was demolished in 1895. The citizens of Paducah looked forward to a new era with the completion of Morton's Opera House, which would seat 1,100. An air of growing expectancy followed the periodic reports on the progress of the structure. Brickwork was finished on August 13, 1884, and an announcement on September 26 indicated that the building soon would be ready. Finally, on November 10, Miss Patti Rose's Opera Company opened in "Mizpah" with local talent providing the music for the first performance.

Fire claimed Morton's in 1900. A new and more elegant theater, The Kentucky Theater, replaced it. This was built at a cost of $60,000 and could seat 1,600. The structure was located on north Fifth between Broadway and Jefferson Streets. The occasion of the grand opening was tinged with sadness. President McKinley died on September 14, and Paducah still mourned his assassination. Nevertheless, the city planned a gala benefit for September 24, 1901. Tickets for the opening went high. Orchestra seats cost $5, as did the first five rows of the balcony. The rest of the balcony cost $3. The first three rows of the gallery sold for $2, the remainder for $1.50 each. Herbert Cawthorne and a troop of 80 presented *The Burgomaster*, a play based upon the biography of Peter Stuyvesant of New Amsterdam.

Besides the theater, Paducahans enjoyed a wide variety of other types of entertainment. The Germania Singing Society at Lehrer's Hall performed a grand musical in 1874. Parades, cornet bands, and lodges counted for many bright moments in an otherwise drab period; however, the Hook and Ladder Company and the Paducah Silver Cornet Band had to postpone one parade due to muddy streets. The coming of the new street railroad made band concerts and excursions popular. A pinwheel and band concert was held at Bellevue Garden on July 4, 1877. The festive events were capped by a balloon ascent. Beer, ice cream, and the music of James Fitch's string band kept the crowd happy.

Among the Episcopalians, musical gatherings and ice cream socials were frequent in the 1870s and 1880s to raise money to pay for the new Grace Church

A big event in the late 1930s was the strawberry festival with its parade and the crowning of a queen. (Courtesy MHM.)

building. In a letter from Frannie Rabb to her sister Mary on February 2, 1873, Frannie reported that "Mr. Leopold's concert and Mrs. Pickett's charade came off in both of which I take part. The charade is for the benefit of the church parish Aid Society. It is going to be in Mrs. Pickett's parlour. She herself is going to recite a piece." Fannie wished she could prevail upon Mrs. Pickett to dance the Highland fling.

Sometimes, the socials were organized by business firms to foster sales. An advertisement in the *Paducah Daily News* on May 28, 1879, announced that Mrs. Harris, proprietor of the Mineral Well, would give a moonlight party on the following evening for "young ladies and gentlemen only." Croquet was in vogue for the active. Two swings were available for cozy conversations. Strawberries and ice cream would be served to all. Steamboat cruises also were popular in the period. During the summer of 1879, one could ride from Paducah to Cairo on the *James Fisk Jr.* or the *Champion* and return. Two meals were included in the fare of a quarter.

Young boys had different ideas of entertainment. The slow-moving streetcars were objects of pranks on more than one occasion. Once, bricks were placed on the tracks on Locust Street (now Third Street). The driver did not see them and was thrown over the front of his car. Fortunately for him, the car did not run up on him nor did the mule show his objection to the new arrangement. Nevertheless, Pat Halloran, manager of the line, expressed concern and urged parents to discourage the practice. A similar prank took place on Broadway just in front of the American German National Bank nine years later. A railroad signal torpedo was placed on the car tracks and went undetected until the car passed over it. The resulting explosion caused the driver and passengers to tumble out of the car while the employees of the bank, thinking they were being attacked by desperados, appeared in the doorway with cocked pistols. One bystander commented that he was reminded of Forrest's raid.

Much of the entertainment in Paducah centered in the home. The piano became the focus of the family gatherings (at least until the 1937 flood) and music lessons were a must for proper Paducahans. An advertisement dated September 25, 1879, announced that Miss Purington planned to resume teaching in September. Mr. V. Eisenman offered voice lessons and instrumental instruction at the same time. Twenty weeks of instruction in a class of two cost $25 or $30 for private lessons. For those not able to generate music from a pump organ or a piano, the player piano and the Edison phonograph proved to be a boon. Mrs. C.L. Rieke put her new Edison phonograph on public display, and then invited a select group to a private party that featured Italian and American opera, band, and orchestra selections. She also had one cylinder of literary recitations.

Those seeking access to the latest intellectual advancements in early 1908 could attend the summer Chautauqua sessions. The papers in Paducah announced on June 13, 1909, that Williams Jennings Bryan would be the principal speaker at the Chautauqua. The fact that Bryan had been the candidate for the Democratic Party for president in 1896, 1900, and 1908 guaranteed interest and attendance at the vespers hour of 4:00 p.m.

Paducah entered the twentieth century with optimism and one of the first electric trolley systems in Kentucky. Young boys sometimes disrupted the system with pranks. (Courtesy SB.)

America's favorite pastime was alive and well in Paducah too. The city's first Kitty League ball team was called the Paducah Indians. (Courtesy JSJ.)

Bryan's topic was "The Prince of Peace." The report of the speech gave the reason for Bryan's choice of topic:

> Mr. Bryan said that he had persuaded himself to write and lecture out of the sole desire to do the youth and the young men of the land some good, in disabusing their minds of many of the isms and schisms so many turn to or are led into through college lives, having a tendency to wander away from the teachings of their fathers and mothers and delve into the theories of creation, the science of life, and other similar mysteries which no man has yet solved and which no man can or will solve.

Bryan initiated his attack on evolution in this speech. In his audience was the family of John Thomas Scopes, who later was the center of the famous "Monkey Trials" in Dayton, Tennessee, in which Bryan helped prosecute Scopes.

The arrival of a circus was occasion for celebration—most of the time. Smith's Great American Circus arrived in Paducah in 1857, and Dan Rice appeared in 1870. John Robinson set up his show on the Bynd property on south Third Street and played to an estimated 3,000 patrons one afternoon in 1888. However, the Buffalo Bill Wild West Show seemed to have hit a particular responsive chord in Paducah. Opening November 18, 1884, the cowboy show was an immediate hit. Large crowds pressed forward to watch the daring riders, and youth in the town

The popular Columbia Theater, which opened in 1927, was one of the first in the nation to boast air conditioning. The electric sign was 50 feet tall and required 5,000 lightbulbs. (Courtesy MHM.)

tried to imitate the heroes of the West. Buffalo Bill returned to Paducah on more than one occasion and in fact, Paducah became the home of a rival to Mr. Cody's show. Fletcher Terrell created the Buckskin Bill Wild West Show, which claimed to be surpassed only by the Cody show and that of Pawnee Bill. Wagons and equipment of the troupe wintered in Paducah and its vicinity.

Around the same time, Paducahans began to throw off their ties to the steel rails and seek adventure on the open road. Dr. J.D. Robertson accepted delivery of an Oldsmobile on November 2, 1901, and other cars followed in rapid succession. On June 14, 1904, a shipment of Fords arrived at Foreman Brothers and made front-page news. Increasing use of the new vehicles quickly led to abuse. The City of Paducah reacted to the presence of the automobile by enacting an ordinance requiring all automobiles to have bells and lights. The speed was limited to 8 miles per hour. Violation of the ordinance led to fines ranging from $5 to $50. More powerful engines made the new machines more attractive and soon, small cars surpassed the 12-horsepower capability of the electric streetcars of the time.

An automobile club formed in Paducah. On August 8, 1904, the second expedition of members and guests of the Paducah Auto Club set forth for Lovelaceville. An hour and fifteen minutes later, the party arrived. After a rest and a picnic, the caravan packed up and left at 2:00 p.m. On the return trip, Will Reike and L.B. Ogilvie were hurt when their Ford skidded off the road and overturned.

The City Commission took notice of the increased number of automobiles. On May 23, 1905, an ordinance decreed that all such vehicles had to be numbered and licensed. A lower speed limit also was considered. Change often provokes angry responses and such was the case with the introduction of the automobile in Paducah. A growing animosity between drivers of the new vehicles and the police made a clash inevitable; however, it was postponed for a while by accommodation. The Paducah Automobile Club persuaded the City to rope off Third Street between Broadway and Jefferson for two or three consecutive days in September. During these periods, drivers could pit their machines against each other and enjoy the sense of exhilaration that seems to the average American to be a byproduct of exhaust fumes. The City could not continue to cater to racers, and the drivers would not restrain the urge to press the gas pedal to the floor. Sober citizens protested speeding in the city.

City police prepared to cope with the growing threat of speeders on the streets and the City began an elaborate program to contain the menace. This involved using the very latest in scientific equipment to apprehend violators of the city ordinances. Stopwatches were purchased and tested. On June 22, 1909, 11 warrants were issued to some of the most promising youth of the community. They received fines for speeds approaching 18 miles per hour. All was not lost, however, as the drivers insisted that the existing speed limit was not reasonable. On July 13, the speed limit was raised to 15 miles per hour everywhere except in the business district, where 10 miles per hour prevailed.

Horse racing in Paducah dates at least from the year after the Civil War. This track at Carson Park was popular at the turn of the twentieth century. (Courtesy Blalock/Stacey Families.)

Harness racing at Carson Park was and still is popular in Paducah. (Courtesy JJ.)

Kentuckians are known for their predilection to horse racing. In various forms this sport has amused Paducahans at least since 1866. A fair became an annual event for McCracken County during the summer and continues to include racing (except from 1942 to 1945). People flocked to Paducah by boat and rail to a track on Old Mayfield Road (this site was demolished in 1899). Carson Park at Twenty-ninth and Jefferson built a half-mile track that accommodated both racing and horse shows. Wooden seating was replaced in 1985 with a modern metal structure seating 3,000. It appeared that Paducah had made a coup with the announcement that a thoroughbred racetrack would be built on the west side of the city.

Racing began in 1984 with quarter horse races. The new venture was hit with 30 days of rain. Coupled with the soft, new track, the rain led to broken legs, reduced attendance, and financial disaster. A new group of local investors took over in 1987 and changed the name to Bluegrass Downs. A major change was the advent of thoroughbred racing. In 1993, Players bought the Paducah track to accompany their casino on the river at Metropolis, Illinois. Both live racing and simulcast events were available. However, the attendance did not live up to projections. As a result, the track was sold and now is Harrah's, offering standard bred and harness racing plus simulcast events from other tracks.

Bawdy houses provided Paducahans and visitors with a great deal of entertainment. Being a river town, the city always had a reputation for rowdiness. The newspapers carried lurid accounts of fights, raids, and disturbances in the bordellos. Vicarious titillation by journalists was expected and tolerated until the reputation of the city got out of hand. Prostitution in Paducah attracted many to the town including steamboat crews, drummers, conventioneers, and soldiers.

The last two decades of the nineteenth century saw a burst of growth in Paducah. A new post office was completed in 1885 and the new city hall opened two years earlier. Reliable access to pure water became a given after 1886 and night was subdued with the completion of a city gas plant that offered fuel for the 300 lamps set on 9-foot posts throughout the city. City streets were renamed in 1886, with numbered cross streets replacing the previous use of tree names. Still, the city retained much of its rough frontier heritage. A cow grazed on the courthouse lawn. Bennett & Company's city directory reported that Paducah, the "Plain City," had 20 churches and 5 banks. However, the same directory contained a list of 54 saloons and 13 establishments that also sold wine.

A wave of reform slowly gained momentum as revivals stimulated the religious community into action. A revival conducted by Dixon O. "Dixie" Williams in a tent during the summer of 1890 provoked a sensation in Paducah. The last session on September 14 drew more than 3,500 perspiring penitents. This is remarkable, as the 1890 census reported Paducah had a population of 14,000. Many churches continued to hold "protracted" meetings throughout the rest of the year. The local newspaper noted on September 20 that "Paducah has never perhaps witnessed such a religious interest as has prevailed here as stated, and it looks now as if it is to continue some time without relaxing a great deal."

This city hall was built in 1883 and the top floor added in 1909. (Courtesy SB.)

In 1905, a new wave of revivals began, started by the Baptists in November 1904, when George T. Gates, a minister from Louisville, embarked on the venture. The paper cited the end of the marathon event in a report on February 8. It noted that more than 1,000 conversions took place and approximately 700 joined the various churches. Flocks swelled in many congregations and Paducah enjoyed a season of religious regeneration and rejoicing. Spurred by the desire to rid the city of immoral practices, reformers took action. By 1916, Paducah changed dramatically.

After a flood and a homecoming celebration in 1913, Paducah tackled the problem of prostitution again. The leader of this movement was Clinton S. Quin, the new rector of Grace Episcopal Church. In one of the 57 diaries kept by Quin, he described Paducah as being "like ancient Damascas [*sic*], and Sodom and Gomorrah." To Quin, the city "was a trading city; the host of countless drummers and, therefore, the provender of appropriate entertainment." Quin also noted in his journal that Paducah was without a levee: "a high town beyond the danger of floods." Paducah also was in need of something for boys to do. Quin founded one of the first Boy Scout troops in the nation in 1910. Troop One was joined by Troop Nine on October 1, 1917, at Fountain Avenue Methodist Church.

From the great reform effort of 1916 to the present, prostitution has kept a low profile in Paducah. One or two houses continued to provide for community needs and received tacit acceptance. During the boom in the early 1950s and into the early 1960s, the two houses closed; however, Paducah gained the reputation of being a good liberty town for servicemen, especially from Fort Campbell. City leaders encouraged this image. Such an act of toleration can lead to embarrassing moments for city officials. In the late 1990s, one house on South Third caused the city fire marshal, allegedly a frequent patron who used his position to gain favors without pay, to resign.

Pictured here is the pioneer Boy Scout Troop One of Paducah. (Courtesy Bill Black Jr.)

14. Bending the Color Line

Treatment of African Americans in Paducah followed a pattern that was not uncommon in much of the nation. In 1908, Ray Stannard Baker wrote *Following the Color Line*, an investigation of segregation in America. Baker noted the increase in lynching and tried to explain such acts of violence in terms "of the distrust of the Southern white man of his own judicial process." Certainly fear of violence and displays of violence played a role in the reduction of blacks to second-class status prior to 1900, but there was more.

Conditions in Paducah were not dissimilar from those in the nation at large. Between 1872 and 1916, African Americans were courted for their votes but relegated to second-class status as citizens. On October 23, 1883, the Paducah *Daily News* reported that "a colored barber" tried to sit in the section reserved for whites in the St. Clair Hall. He was ejected, much to the paper's delight. Newspapers frequently objected to the boisterous behavior of bootblacks on Broadway in Paducah in the last years of the nineteenth century. The *Daily News* for October 28, 1889, branded these African Americans as "young hoodlums" and urged the city authorities to run them out of the downtown area. A previous issue reported that daughters of whites were offended by the "ribald and obscene" language of the bootblacks and, as a result, "couldn't shop." As was often the case, racial persecution was presented as moral reform.

Paducahans could be proud of the accomplishments of local blacks, but unfortunately, it was a patronizing pride. One such example is Henry H. Urquhart, who was paid $9,000 for a patent on a brake shoe for steam engines in 1906. At the time, Urquhart worked as a switchman on the Illinois Central.

Race relations in Paducah reached their lowest point in 1916. Luther Durrett and Brack Kinley were lynched on October 16. Kinley was accused of raping a white woman on the Pool Road and had been put into the county jail. A mob gathered and, despite the brave and determined resistance of Judge William Reed, took Kinley from the jail. Armed with a pistol, Durrett followed the crowd, muttering threats to the mob of whites. He was seized and forced to go along to the house of the woman involved. There, Kinley was identified and both men were hanged, shot, and burned. Five thousand people were said to have witnessed the event.

Judge Reed branded the lynch mob murderers and called for a special grand jury to investigate the incident. For his effort, Reed received the commendation

THE NEWS-DEMOCRAT.

"The Paper That Is Growing With Paducah"

VOL. 50., NO. 249. PADUCAH, KENTUCKY, TUESDAY MORNING, OCTOBER 17, 1916. 12¢ A WEEK; 5¢ A COPY

MOB HANGS NEGRO RAPIST AND ANOTHE[R] NEGRO WHO SAID HE WOULD FIRE INTO [...]

RUMANIANS ARE HOLDING BACK TEUTON FORCE

ARMY HEADQUARTERS CLAIMS THEY HAVE TAKEN SEVERAL POSITIONS FROM GERMANS IN THE ALT RIVER REGION.

EAST FRONT IS RAGING

MASTER BAKERS GATHER FOR TWO DAY CONVENTION

FIRST BUSINESS SESSION OPENS THIS MORNING AT 9:30 AT KNIGHTS OF COLUMBUS HALL —IMPORTANT DEBATE.

200 DELEGATES EXPECTED

LYCEUM TO GIVE HEATH PROGRAM TONIGHT, 7:30

NUMBERS OF PRESS CONCERT TO BE GIVEN BY BOTH HEATH AND PADUCAH TALENT—SECOND OF ENTERTAINMENTS.

THIRD CONCERT FRIDAY

ILLICIT LOVERS ARE FOUND DEAD LYING IN FIELD

THREE BULLET HOLES ARE IN THE BREAST OF 14-YEAR-OLD ELMA COPE—ONE IN HEART OF HARLEY BROWN, 24.

GIRL'S BROTHER-IN-LAW

VOLUNTEERS SAY THEY WILL WORK HARD FOR WILSON

DELEGATION OF INDEPENDENTS SAY THEY FEEL THE PRESIDENT HAS GIVEN THIS NATION A "SQUARE DEAL."

VISIT AT SHADOW LAWN

FIVE THOUSAND PEOPLE SEE EXECUTION AND BURNING [OF] NEGROES BY ENRAGED HO[...]

Brack Kinley, the Rapist, Is Twice Identified by George D. Rose, As the Negro Who Ass[aulted] Her at Her Home on the Pool Road.

COUNTY JAIL IS BESIEGED BY OVER A THOUSAND MEN FOR ABOUT 3 HO[URS]

Officials Find Themselves Powerless to Do Anything—Judge Comes Near to Death—Pr[ecau]tions Are Taken to Head Off Race Riot.

MOB MAKES NO ATTEMPT AT SEC[...]

The nadir in race relations in Paducah, as reported in the News-Democrat, *was in October 1916, when two men were lynched while a crowd estimated at 5,000 watched. (Courtesy MCCPL.)*

of Governor A.O. Stanley and a warning note from an unknown Paducahan. On the same day that Governor Stanley sent his supporting letter to Reed, 75 African Americans left Paducah to work on the B&O Railroad in West Virginia. There is no evidence that the lynching influenced the decision of so many blacks to emigrate, but all no doubt knew of it.

Bad feelings between whites and blacks surfaced again on August 20, 1936. A white employee of the Illinois Central Railroad attended a church picnic at Twenty-eighth and Jefferson and was observed to be slightly intoxicated by several in attendance. Later, J.E. Linn saw a car crash into a utility pole with the driver slumped over. Linn recognized the driver and rushed to get assistance. The 48-year-old driver reached the Illinois Central Hospital at 1501 Broadway alive but soon bled to death. The body bore three stab wounds, including the fatal cut on the left arm that severed an artery. The victim was from an old Paducah family and left a wife and four children. The funeral at St. Francis de Sales Roman Catholic Church at Sixth and Broadway was a community event.

Two days later, Rex Cornelison, the city judge, announced that a black male youth of 19 had been arrested on August 21 on a murder warrant. Even before a trial, Joe Hale was rushed to Eddyville prison for safekeeping. An all-white jury found Hale guilty and he received a sentence of death in the electric chair.

Witnesses testified that Hale had recently returned from reform school. While visiting a relative, he alleged that his group saw a white man drive past the house in the 700 block of Jackson Street. Hale, according to witnesses, said that "this is the man who has been stopping colored women and asking them to get in his car; I know his car." With that, Hale hurriedly left. When he returned, Hale allegedly said, "that man went up Ohio Street and parked in the dark. I 'gigged' him a time or two and told him to quit stopping these colored women."

Hale did not think he had hurt him badly. His white attorneys appealed Hale's case to the U.S. Supreme Court from Paducah, led by a relative of Colonel Crossland, who was wounded in the assault on Fort Anderson when Forrest raided Paducah in 1864. Others helped present the case including Charles R. Houston and Leon A. Ransom from the District of Columbia, who argued the appeal before the highest tribunal on March 29, 1938, with assistance from Edward P. Lovell, also from the District, and Thurgood Marshall of Baltimore, Maryland. Hale's attorneys argued that his conviction should be overturned when it was established that all qualified blacks were excluded from the grand jury and petit jury solely on account of race while the federal district court in Paducah did not make such exclusion. No blacks served on state juries between 1906 and 1936.

Counsel contended they could prove a "long, continued, unvarying and wholesale exclusion of Negroes from jury service in this County on account of their race and color." This act constituted a denial of the equal protection of the laws guaranteed to a petitioner by the Fourteenth Amendment.

Eleven men had been executed at Eddyville while Hale's appeal was pending. Hale waited 32 months and 5 days. Paducah papers tended to ignore the case. The decision reached on May 15, 1938, merited a mention on page three of the local newspaper. Hale was re-tried on April 25, 1939, convicted of a lesser crime, and received a life sentence. He reportedly said, "I was pretty proud to get what I did."

The case made a ripple, not a wave, in racism. McCracken County officials ignored the ruling successfully until 1954, when Joseph Freeland, attorney

This detail from Paducah's floodwall mural by Robert Dafford reflects the joy of the African-American homecoming (August 8) event in the 1870–1900 era.

Paducah was also known as a place of prayer. Shown here is Burks' Chapel with its African-American congregation. (Courtesy Mrs. T.G. Munday.)

representing Curlee Brown, president of the local chapter of the NAACP, filed what was a pioneer use of affirmative action to force McCracken County to impanel blacks. Federal District Court Judge Roy Shelbourne agreed not to issue the requested injunction even though it was warranted when the county officials agreed to comply with the dictates of the U.S. Supreme Court and put African Americans on jury panels.

After the end of the Second World War, Paducah became a target city in the effort of the NAACP to improve the condition of black students in Kentucky. Mixing of races in school classrooms was not legal in Kentucky at the time.

Curlee Brown of the NAACP reported in an interview with Glen Murrell in 1967 that the organization decided to take action against Paducah Junior College in 1948. The college was publicly supported and was subject to the provisions of the Day Law prohibiting the mixing of races in schools. Further, the white students could take two years of college work at PJC. Blacks in Paducah did not have equal opportunity for a college education comparable to that of whites.

On September 12, 1949, Lee Powell and Joseph S. Freeland, attorney for the NAACP in Paducah, appeared at PJC seeking admission. Dean Matheson of PJC examined Powell's credentials and his request for admission was denied—not on the basis of race but due to unacceptable scholarship.

The following day, Freeland reappeared with Fred A. Wilson Jr. The college authorities had either to accept his application or obey the existing law. Wilson was refused admission because of his race. As a result, a suit was filed in U.S. District Court at Paducah.

The local legal staff of the NAACP received valuable assistance in preparing the case from Thurgood Marshall (later, the first black associate justice of the U.S. Supreme Court) and Robert Carter of the NAACP's Legal Defense and Education Funds Inc. As a result, the City of Paducah was added to the suit as a defendant since it contributed tax monies to the college.

After legal maneuvering, the NAACP decided to retreat from a direct attack on the Day Law and attempted to prove that the doctrine of "separate but equal" education was violated in Paducah. The first true college in the Jackson Purchase was West Kentucky Industrial College, founded in 1907 by Dr. D.H. Anderson, who moved his "normal" school for training black teachers from Mayfield to Paducah. This school provided black teachers with the required courses to teach in the public schools. The school also became the center of cultural and social activities in the African-American community. The college functioned as a teacher training normal school until 1938, when its college level courses moved to Kentucky State in Frankfort.

Judge Roy Shelbourne ruled on October 27, 1950, "qualified colored students had the right to attend Paducah Junior College." One immediate consequence of this ruling was that the University of Louisville opened its doors to African Americans. The Day Law was modified in 1950 to allow coeducation of whites and blacks in public or private school above the high school level if comparable courses were not then available at Kentucky State in Frankfort. PJC appealed the decision and continued to refuse admission to blacks.

An era ended with the graduation of the last class at Western Kentucky Industrial College in 1938. The institution was turned into a vocational school for post–high school African-American students. (Courtesy MHM.)

On January 22, 1952, the federal court in Paducah "enjoining and restraining the college from excluding qualified Negroes" issued a mandatory injunction. Again PJC appealed. The United States Court of Appeals for the Sixth Circuit at Cincinnati found against PJC on February 2, 1953. Further appeal by the college ended. On June 9, 1953, four blacks enrolled at the college without incident. Integration had arrived in Paducah.

The city was more fortunate than other towns in Kentucky in that integration came without violence. The National Guard unit from Paducah was called into active duty to prevent trouble in Sturgis, 68 miles northeast of Paducah in Union County. The leadership in Paducah should be commended for its constructive approach to integration. Both black and white factions refrained from creating an environment based on crises. The control over public opinion exercised by the Paxton family proved to be helpful in this connection. While not censoring the news, the paper and television exercised restraint in how news was slanted; thus moderating conditions that could have gotten out of hand.

One significant influence in promoting peaceful integration was the Non-Partisan League. W.G. Harvey wrote Mayor Robert Cherry on February 28, 1963, protesting the continued presence of "Jim Crow" signs (that indicated separate sections based on race) at local movie theaters. The letter concluded "we believe that progress in a city depends on the progress in civil rights, and we need a combination of efforts to take care of this matter, for we would like to do this peacefully and religiously."

Harvey's letter was passed on to Robert P. Petter, a member of the Mayor's Committee on Human Rights. Petter wrote Harvey on March 13 and reported, "I was told at our Committee meeting last night that the sign at the Arcade Theater had been removed. We ourselves did not speak to Mr. [Jack] Keiler about the signs because there are negotiations going on regarding the de-segregation of the theaters and we felt the signs would take care of themselves once de-segregation was achieved."

The Non-Partisan League sent out a special announcement: "After July 1, 1963, all persons, regardless of race, creed, or color will have access to the South Twin Drive In Theater, and the Sunset Drive in Theater." The announcement also noted that "after Labor Day, all persons will have access to the Paducah Drive In Theater, and after October 3, 1963, all areas and facilities at the Columbia and Arcade Theaters will be available to all persons." The League felt that this was quite an accomplishment and asked that those who chose to take advantage of these facilities should be on their best behavior. This schedule for a gradual integration worked.

Restraint was shown by all concerned. In a letter to John W. Keiler dated June 27, Harvey said, "On behalf of the Non-Partisan League of the Greater Paducah Area, I am happy to inform you that we have not had any undue publicity in the papers as you requested." A copy of the special announcement was enclosed, referring to the suggestion about good behavior.

W.G. Harvey was the first African American to preside over a meeting of the Paducah City Commission. (Courtesy Reverend W.G. Harvey.)

The Non-Partisan League worked with city officials to improve the chances for employment of African Americans in municipal jobs. The approach was low-key, but effective. Mayor Cherry wrote the chairman of the Water and Power Boards suggesting that since blacks made up 16.7 percent of the city's population, a similar ratio should exist in employment practices. The League thanked the mayor in a letter dated June 27, 1963.

African Americans began to be appointed to important civic boards during the 1960s. Harvey, Wilber Lee, W.C. Young, and other young men in the city became recognized as Paducah leaders instead of "important blacks." Mayor Tom Wilson named Harvey to the city housing commission, breaking a precedent that had kept all Paducah boards white. The board of commissioners approved Harvey's nomination unanimously.

The appointment of Harvey to fill a vacancy on the city board of commissioners by Mayor Robert Cherry also broke another color line. Harvey had been the runner-up in the recent election, losing by a very narrow margin. The death of an incumbent on the commission allowed Cherry to select the candidate next in line, Harvey. Soon afterward, George Chancellor reported "Harvey Conducts Commission Meet" in the *Paducah Sun-Democrat*: "Saying simply, 'Would you call the roll, please?' The Reverend W.G. Harvey, a Negro, convened the first meeting of the Paducah City Commission to be presided over by a member of his race Tuesday night." Wilber Lee, the lone African-American on the Paducah Planning and Zoning Commission, expressed the sentiments of the black community on the history-making occasion: "I'm a proud black Paducahan tonight."

The color line still exists, but it has been altered. Significant gains have been made, but much remains to be done. The remarkable thing is that the community could work out divisive problems without critical crises developing. Paducah should be both thankful and proud.

15. Politics: 1937–2000

Before 1937, Paducah played only a small role in national politics. Charles K. Wheeler caused eyebrows to raise when he went to Washington as a presidential elector from Kentucky in the election of 1892. What caused interest was not the unique opportunity to vote in the election of the only man to serve a split term as President, fellow Democrat Grover Cleveland, but rather that Wheeler did not protest the election of another to a federal post he thought might be his. This selfless trait was noted earlier in 1884, when Cleveland said of him, "That must be a good sort of man to tie to."

Wheeler served as the congressman of the First District from 1897 until 1903. While in office, Wheeler caught the nation's attention with a passionate protest against what he considered "flunkeyism and toadyism" on the part of the administration and the State Department. Xenophobic in tone, his speech reflected the growing anti-foreign feelings of many in the nation. At issue was a reception for a brother of the German Kaiser and the pending trip of Alice Roosevelt, the daughter of President Theodore Roosevelt, to attend the coronation of Edward VII of the United Kingdom. Earlier, Wheeler attempted to block the Republican efforts to assist the Cuban people in their attempt to gain freedom from Spain. Charles Wheeler retired after two terms and made the following comments:

> I would not advise anybody to enter politics unless he is very poor or very rich. If very poor, he has not much to lose, providing he can ward off attacks on his character, and that is one of the most distressing features of politics, to malign in general. If he is rich he has a better chance of enjoying his experience—yet it is an experience that no one can regret, except for the financial loss and the enemies he makes.

Wheeler returned to his law practice, which once employed a young clerk named Alben Barkley.

On the national scene, Alben William Barkley, an adopted Paducahan, began to attract favorable notice from the leaders of the Democratic Party and from the nation at large after his dramatic keynote address to the nominating convention at Chicago in 1932, which opted to back Franklin D. Roosevelt for president. In that speech, Barkley coined the phrase "a New Deal" as a cure for the economic

Paducah's Alben Barkley created the modern office of Vice President of the United States after he and Harry S. Truman won a stunning victory in 1948. Shown here with Mrs. Truman, the two men (front row) are boarding the "Sacred Cow," the plane that began the tradition of designated airplanes for both the President and the Vice President of the United States (Courtesy MHM.)

woes that had all but strangled trade and commerce since 1929. Barkley also assisted Senate leader Joseph T. Robinson in guiding a spate of innovative reform legislation through the first 90 days of the new Congress that met in 1933. Roosevelt developed such confidence in Barkley that he asked him to repeat as the key speaker at the 1936 convention re-nominating Roosevelt for a second term. Upon Robinson's death in 1937, Barkley moved into the leadership of the Senate in what proved to be one of the most trying periods in the history of the nation.

Barkley and Roosevelt did not always agree. Barkley insisted on a tax measure that Roosevelt vetoed. As a result, Barkley resigned his post as leader in the Senate. This led to a series of "Dear Alben" letters from the President, which led Barkley to return to the vital post he held in the Senate during the difficult days of World War II. Barkley's quick reelection set a precedent of autonomy for future congressional leaders. Be that as it may, Roosevelt picked Truman to run as vice president rather than Barkley in 1944.

In 1948, Barkley again set the tone for the convention of the Democratic Party. At the time, few political analysts gave the Democrats a chance of winning against the popular Republican Governor Thomas Dewey of New York. Truman, as presidential candidate, and Barkley, seeking the vice presidency, took their cause

Alben Barkley's grandson nicknamed Barkley, "the Veep," and the name stuck.

directly to the people. Truman used a private railroad car on his "whistle stop" tour noted for his "give 'em hell, Harry" ad lib remarks from the back platform of his coach. Barkley used a surplus Air Force bomber to flit from city to city in a whirlwind tour belying his age. Together, they pulled off one of the most unexpected victories in American politics.

On January 29, 1949, at the age of 72, Barkley took the oath of office as vice president—the oldest man to do so. Dorothy Brower of Tiptonville, Tennessee, Barkley's first wife, died in 1947. The nation watched with both amusement and admiration as Barkley courted Jane Rucker Hadley of St. Louis. They married January 30, 1949, making Barkley the only vice president to marry while in office. Barkley also was the first working vice president. Previously, the vice president presided over the Senate. Barkley, at Truman's insistence, took an active part in the meetings of the cabinet and the National Security Council. During his tenure, the office of vice president also acquired its own flag, marking it as one of the vital components of the national government.

Barkley made an active bid for his party's nomination for president in 1952. His age (75) proved to be a disadvantage. He turned instead to hosting a show on national television. Still, the political scene called. In 1954, Barkley handily upset the incumbent Republican senator, John Sherman Cooper. Although now a junior senator, Barkley received an appointment to the prestigious Senate Foreign Relations Committee.

Active and involved, he could not resist attending a mock convention held by the students at Washington and Lee University. After ending his speech there with the observation that he "would rather be a servant in the house of the Lord than to sit in the seats of the mighty," Barkley died of a massive heart attack. His funeral brought Harry S. Truman and many other dignitaries to Paducah. The former President stayed at the Irvin S. Cobb Hotel and walked up and across the street to the Broadway Methodist Church for the funeral.

At the state level, Paducah contributed several leaders that helped mold and redefine the government of the commonwealth. Kentucky's Constitution of 1891 is a quaint relic that reflected the attitudes of a people before the advent of the automobile and most of modern culture. Still it remains, like the albatross of the ancient mariner. Tom Waller, a Paducah attorney, attempted to unshackle the state from its past by suggesting that a constitutional convention be called since the present instrument could only be changed by an arduous process of putting two items before the people in a general election. Little came of this other than to awake the population to the need for change in the existing system, particularly the judiciary. It fell to Julian Carroll, another Paducah attorney and politician, to accomplish the reform of Kentucky's court system.

A resident of Heath, near Paducah, Julian Morton Carroll took an associate of arts degree from Paducah Junior College in 1952 and went on to the University of Kentucky for his law degree in 1956. After a stint in the military, Carroll began to practice law in Paducah, where he also taught part time at the college. In 1961, Carroll won the first of six terms as a member of the Kentucky House.

The marker dedicated to "Veep" Barkley is located at Twenty-eighth and Jefferson Streets.

Julian Carroll grew up in Heath and attended Paducah Junior College, where he later taught, and the University of Kentucky. He became a power in Frankfort in the general assembly, won election as governor, and oversaw the reform of the state judiciary.

From 1968 until 1970, Carroll directed the House as its Speaker. In 1971, Bert Combs picked Carroll to run for lieutenant governor to assure that far western Kentucky would support the candidacy of the eastern Kentuckian Combs. While Combs lost to fellow Democrat Wendell Ford, Carroll won the party nomination and was elected. Ford opted to resign as governor and moved to the U.S. Senate on December 28, 1974, making Carroll governor. In 1975, Carroll got strong support to run again and easily defeated Republican Robert E. Gable by 453,210 to 274,559. While governor, Carroll pushed educational reform of the public schools. He also started the state Department of Energy, as coal was in great demand at the time due to the oil embargo of the Oil Producing and Exporting Countries (OPEC).

Carroll, the first governor of Kentucky from the Purchase area, had "an extensive knowledge of the details of government," according to Attorney Mark C. Whitlow. As a result, he could micromanage legislation. "A cockroach couldn't crawl across the Senate floor without an OK from the governor stamped on his back," Whitlow wrote. Thus, Carroll managed quietly to get a constitutional amendment passed in 1975 that allowed him to revamp the state's court system. The position of county judge lost its judicial function and became administrative. The Court of Appeals, the state's highest court, was renamed the Supreme Court. A new Court of Appeals was to hear appeals from the circuit courts. City courts were abolished and new district courts took over.

Several Paducahans achieved seats on the new higher courts. Judge Brady Stewart won election to the Court of Appeals in 1951 and served until 1967 and

Roy Vance, a special commissioner on the Court of Appeals, became one of the judges on the new Court of Appeals. Later, in 1983, Vance won a seat on the Supreme Court of Kentucky. Former city attorney and city manager J. William Howerton won election to the new Appeals Court in 1976, became chief justice from December 1986 through 1990, and retired after 20 years on the bench in November 1996. In 1995, J.W. "Bill" Graves won a seat on the Supreme Court for an unexpired term and was re-elected in 1996.

Women became a political force in Paducah in 1919. In fact, they played a significant role in their first election as the question of selling bonds to fund the construction of Augusta Tilghman High School and Lincoln High School was on the ballot. There were 2,291 women registered and they constituted 46 percent of the electorate. The two parties were almost equally represented: 2,657 Democrats and 2,283 Republicans.

In 1923, Frances Allen became the first woman to hold an elected office in Paducah when the Democrat won the office of treasurer. In 1943, Wayne Seaton defeated Mary Dorian in the race for the mayor's office by 3,497 to 2,710. It remained for Mrs. Houston "Dolly" McNutt to put a woman in charge of the city in 1971. Also in that election, Clifford Robinson was the first African-American candidate for mayor. Dolly carried 22 of 28 precincts and tied for another.

Alice "Dolly" McNutt became the first woman to serve as mayor of a second-class city in Kentucky. (Courtesy Paducah Sun.*)*

Blacks played an important role in Paducah politics after the 1870s. They functioned as a part of Hazelip's successful machine in the years just prior to World War I and often provided the decisive factor in turning elections to the Republicans until the 1920s, after which time their influence declined. This trend changed when W.G. Harvey became the first African-American man to serve on the city commission. In 1969, Harvey garnered more votes than any other commissioner and thus became the city's first black mayor pro tempore. Robert Coleman became a commissioner during the term of Dolly McNutt and, with one exception, has served to 2000. His experience is a valued asset to the city administration.

McNutt was noted as a speaker and remembered for her honesty. During her term, Paducah enjoyed federal revenue sharing that allowed for many public improvements. In addition, the City received grants to improve sewers and sewage treatment facilities. New water, power, and sewers went out to the area of Kentucky Oaks Mall and out Coleman Road. The pension funds of both the police and fire departments were funded fully under this administration. Breaking a long period of declining industries, Hubelein opened a plant in Paducah to produce vodka. A joint city-county landfill opened with assistance and encouragement from the Environmental Protection Agency as the site was to be converted into a park when filled.

The election of George Jacobs as mayor in 1955 was unique, as he had no opposition. It was during the term of Jacobs that a Paducah icon came into being: the Duke of Paducah. Initially, the term applied to Irvin S. Cobb, according to

The family no longer operates Wallerstein's, but the building still carries images of Barkley and Cobb and has been restored recently.

editor Jack Paxton of the *Paducah Sun-Democrat* on May 20, 1979. In Paxton's writing, Cobb was staying at the hotel bearing his name while back in Paducah in the 1940s. Cobb and Fred Neuman, a linotype operator and old friend of Cobb who later wrote one of the better biographies of him, heard a radio program featuring a character called the "Duke of Paducah." Later, Cobb agreed the title should be associated with this performer with a green coat with brass buttons, green hat, high button brogans, rube humor, and the pressing need to "go back to the wagon as these shoes are killin' me." Neuman sent a crate of strawberries, a product Paducah was famous for at the time, to Benjamin Frances Ford, the performer, inviting him to visit Paducah. He did, and he and Neuman became friends. It was Ford that Billie and George Jacobs met at a fair in Metropolis, Illinois, in 1953. Mayor Jacobs told Ford that everywhere he went, people knew of Ford's stage persona and insisted that Ford come to Paducah and accept the title officially. The first Duke of Paducah awards were made late that year to Ford and to Robert Cherry, Wayne C. Smith, Pierce Lackey, and James P. Smith, former mayors.

While the election of Robert Cherry in 1959 certainly was different, it hardly qualifies as unique. Robert Cherry had been mayor in 1951 and had to deal with the influx of thousands of construction workers associated with the gaseous diffusion plant and the two fossil fuel electric generating plants. This rapid increase in population placed severe stress on the infrastructure of the city, but Cherry dealt with the problem in exemplary fashion. In 1959, his friend Richard Fairhurst challenged Cherry. They were members of the same civic organizations but moved in different social cliques. The contest appeared to be the rest of Paducah versus the West End or Cherry versus Fairhurst and the press.

Ultimately the race hinged on challenged votes in one African-American precinct. An attempt was made to seize the machine but James L. Munal, a Republican and an election judge, held his ground until the machine was taken to the courthouse to assure that the votes were valid. The results increased Cherry's lead from 16 to 20 votes. Cherry won election again in 1967. No other mayor has served three four-year terms to date. Cherry tried again in 1975 but lost to William Murphy and in 1979, when John Penrod, a retired FBI agent and teacher of law enforcement at Paducah Community College, won. The principal issue was the need to reform the police department, a task that occupied much of Penrod's term. The only commissioner with prior service at the time was Robert Coleman, also the sole black commissioner. Newcomers included James Flynn, Joe Viterisi, and Harold "Shorty" Ford. Flynn leveraged his experience on the national championship basketball team at UK under Adolph Rupp into political acceptance. Viterisi represented a new force in Paducah, a self-made voice from the north side of the city. Ford, a car salesman and sports enthusiast, parlayed his wide acquaintance within the community into votes.

Tom Wilson served one term as mayor but made a significant contribution by insisting that the city hall remain in the downtown area. Wilson also played a major role in establishing the annual summer festival that continues to draw

Summer Festival founder Mayor Tom Wilson leans out as the flotilla leaves Paducah on the "Ride 'round the Rivers" on July 27, 1975.

crowds to parades, contests, and, for a while, the 80-mile "ride 'round the rivers." Boats left Paducah up the Tennessee to Kentucky Lake, passed through the canal to Lake Barkley, and returned down the Cumberland to the Ohio and on to Paducah. For a time the Coast Guard provided an escort for the flotilla.

Mayor William Murphy completed a project begun under the administration of Dolly McNutt that drastically altered the appearance of the downtown area of Paducah. Project "Townlift" replaced the unsightly utility poles and their myriad wires. He also removed some parking meters that many thought were an impediment to progress that helped turn customers away from the core business district and direct them more toward the suburbs. In his report to the city at the end of his second year in office, Murphy referred to the Townlift project as the "culmination of more than 6-8 years of dreaming, talking and hours and hours of discussion and planning on the part of many dedicated men and women. The modernization of downtown is extremely vital to the continued good health of our entire community. Downtown is the heart of Paducah. That heart must be kept healthy and strong or the entire community will suffer."

In 1979, John Penrod, the former FBI agent and instructor at Paducah Community College, won a bitter race against former mayor Robert Cherry. Penrod faced trying times during his term as mayor. His election platform was a mandate to reform the city jail and the police force. In the process, Penrod appointed Robert Patterson as acting chief. Patterson was the first African American to serve in this capacity, and he served until J.W. Cunningham became chief. (Patterson then later succeeded Cunningham.)

At the beginning of his term, Penrod was fortunate to have James Tidwell as city manager and Carl Holder as an assistant city manager. Shortly after the new commission took office, Tidwell stepped down and Holder took over. It then fell to Penrod to make the final decision on where to locate the new water treatment plant. Various factions advocated the use of deep wells rather than taking water either from the Ohio or the Tennessee. Studies of the feasibility of this approach delayed construction. Finally, Penrod acted and the plant was built on the Ohio. This plant's capacity and efficiency allowed outlying areas to begin tapping on the Paducah system.

Penrod also had to contend with the construction of the Kentucky Oaks Mall, which shifted the center of merchandising and commerce from the core of the downtown area to a spot far to the west of the city limits along the projected Interstate 24 route. The mall wanted to be in the city limits, which required the City to annex a narrow strip along U.S. 45, supply sewer and water lines, and move a fire company to a new location to supply fire protection. Also during Penrod's term, high inflation and declining revenue due to the federal government discontinuing its revenue sharing program forced the City to cut its payroll.

Before Operation Townlift in 1977–1978 cleared away much of the clutter caused by overhead wires in the downtown area, Broadway looked like this. (Courtesy Glen Schrader family.)

Wacinton *by Peter "Wolf" Toth honored the Chickasaw link with Paducah's past.*

Joe Viterisi brought a new perspective into the office of mayor—that of the small businessman. Viterisi ran a neighborhood grocery and lived above the store. He also was the first mayor from either the north or south sides of town. His opponent, Charles Wood, was the retired CEO of one of the large plants located in Calvert City and the former president of the Paducah Area Chamber of Commerce. Wood had the support of the more affluent west end of Paducah. In fact, Wood led in the primary. But Viterisi took his campaign to the voters, registering them in his store and stressing the need to simplify the rules for small businesses. The winning margin was about 400 votes. Viterisi continued a quilt museum project that started during the Penrod era and brought enhanced 911 emergency services to fruition.

Another major accomplishment of this mayor was the implementation of the enterprise zone approach to attracting new business for the city. Viterisi also felt that the purchase of a business license conferred the right to operate a business but did not put a limit on the earnings of a firm, thus ending the city tax on net profits.

Further additions were made to the infrastructure, especially to the sewer system, but personnel problems in the fire department plagued the term of Viterisi, which finally went to the courts for a final determination. Another event that brought a degree of misplaced criticism to Viterisi was his acceptance of the wooden statue of Wacinton by Peter "Wolf" Toth honoring the Chickasaw. Located in front of Noble Park, this 56,000-pound red oak carving is part of Toth's program to place a memorial commemorating the Native Americans in every state in the union.

In 1986, voters approved a constitutional amendment allowing mayors of the state's largest cities to succeed themselves in office. Viterisi became the first candidate to test this new law in the election held in 1987. He seemed to be in a good position, having completed a successful term with the city in better financial condition than when he took office. He had good name recognition and a strong organization. But a surprise candidate emerged saying, "Paducah needs a new enthusiastic leader to put it out of a status quo existence." Geraldine Biggs Montgomery, wife of Dr. Wally Montgomery, a surgeon, and daughter of James Biggs, noted north side supermarket owner, announced that "just to react to problems and maintain status quo is not enough." She promised an active campaign to get more jobs, improve housing, make local neighborhoods safe, renew the downtown and south side areas of town, and provide programs to retain youth in Paducah. Montgomery or her supporters visited every precinct two or three times and she was elected.

Mayor Montgomery began her second day in office with the discovery that the permit for the city landfill had expired and no application had been made for a new one. Also, city hall leaked and, while the previous administration had borrowed more than $1 million to make repairs, close examination disclosed that needed structural alterations were not included in the specifications. Administrative personnel problems requiring her attention also arose early on. Carl Holder, the city manager, left. There was not one computer in city hall. In fact, the only

The waters of Noble Park lake attract ducks and geese all year long.

Albert Jones served the only five-year term as mayor. During his tenure, preservationists and progressives engaged in a running debate about razing relic structures in the older part of the city. (Courtesy Albert Jones.)

computer the City owned was a small mainframe and only one person knew how to use it. The Finance Department was an immediate target for upgrading. As a result, long-term planning had to be delayed but not abandoned.

Montgomery was the first mayor in Paducah to win re-election since it became a second-class city. When the question of a third term arose, she offered her candidacy to continue the programs already under way. Voters had other ideas.

Albert Jones won election to a one-time five-year term as mayor in 1995. Three-and-a-half years into his term, Jones reflected on his administration and on Paducah. His main goal was to deal with demographic change. In each of the last two decades, the census revealed that the city of Paducah lost approximately 3,000 residents. The estimate for 2000 was for another 3,000 emigrants, leaving the population at approximately 26,000. Within that group, 42 percent lived in rented residences. Also, 22 percent were 65 years of age or older. The city school system had four elementary schools. In three of these, between 73 and 83 percent of students were eligible for free or reduced-cost lunches.

Jones also noted that Lynx was the only major employer to come to Paducah in more than a decade. Paducah expanded the number of jobs, but these were in the service industries that pay low wages. The result is a loss of young people and an increase in those who must work two or more jobs to keep up. The role of Paducah as the hub of a market catering to services extends for 150 miles. Jones felt Paducah must do something to attract new jobs that would allow the young people of the city and county to stay in the area and earn reasonable incomes.

To address the demographics, Jones felt that Paducah had to clean out the blight that detracts from potential new industries, and must also supply the necessary infrastructure to allow for future growth, should the population trend change back to increase rather than drain. Enforcement of the existing codes on maintenance was vital. New regulations were now needed to cope with the growth of rental residency. By 1999, 411 derelict structures were razed. Preservationists protested but property owners would not comply voluntarily. This part of Mayor Jones's program was a hot topic for debate.

Jones felt that the continuing close cooperation with the county is vital and must continue; however, he felt that the lack of population at present does not justify an attempt to institute metro government. This might change if people start to relocate to the city again. Nor, he felt, is it cost effective to try to expand by annexation. More than 50 percent of the city budget now goes to police and fire department payrolls. To offer similar services to the county, with its less dense population, would not be cost effective and would require a great increase in county taxes. However, the present trend resulting from the merger of sewer and water services of the city and county may be remembered as one of the most beneficial results of the tenure of Mayor Albert Jones.

This view shows Paducah's city hall from across Dolly McNutt Plaza.

16. Renaissance on the River

As Paducah enters the twenty-first century, opportunities for entertainment widen and become more sophisticated. For example, in 1980, the Paducah Boys' Choir exchanged visits with the world-renowned Vienna Boys' Choir, which returned to Paducah in 2001. The Paducah organization, directed by Tony Whitfield, experienced a revival in 1997 as the Children's Chorus of the Paducah Symphony and the group toured Europe in 1999 and again in 2001. Membership now includes both boys and girls.

The Paducah Symphony continues to improve under the direction of Dr. Jordon Tang while performing in many cities. Dr. Bradley Almquist directs the Symphony Chorus, which visited Prague, Vienna, and Salzburg in concert during 2000. The Paducah Symphony now shares the musical stage with the Paducah Community Band, directed by Doug Van Fleet, during the summer. Van Fleet also directs the Youth Orchestra, which introduces area children to the experience of classical music performances. The symphony features special performances for youth and also sponsors a Young Artist Competition. Winners receive cash prizes for outstanding performances. Competitors are high school students from Missouri, Tennessee, Illinois, New Jersey, and Kentucky.

Paducah Community College began the Lillian Lowry *Focus* series, which brings various performing arts programs to the city along with the continuing community concert series held at Paducah Tilghman Auditorium. In addition, the Market House Theater has earned a fine reputation for the quality of the shows it presents regularly throughout the year.

The William Clark Museum has plans to build a new facility and to leave the middle of the old market house. The Yeiser Art Guild, which has its gallery in the front of the market house, offers a wide menu of media ranging from fabric displays to fine art works. The south end of the market houses the theater, which is reaching capacity and may need a new location before long. The Paducah Area Painters Alliance (PAPA) continues to host shows and presentations of artists in its gallery at 124 Broadway, while Gallery 600 is located five blocks west. A small cadre of artists is in residence in the city.

The Summer Festival, started by Mayor Tom Wilson, gives the city a variety of entertaining events ranging from street bands to classical music performances. Even *National Geographic* took notice of this event in June 1973. During the summer months, the downtown area throbs with music on every street corner

The annual Quilt Show draws over 20,000 visitors to Paducah. Here, Barbara Nitschke displays quilts at the Julian Carroll Convention Center.

on Friday and Saturday nights. A steady stream of automobiles cruises Broadway slowly, with windows down, to listen in and hope to find a rare parking space to stop and participate in the festivities. In July 2001, the press of pedestrians became so pronounced that the City closed lower Broadway to automobiles. A continuous swarm meanders from point to point from late afternoon until past 9:00 p.m.

Fall brings the annual barbecue and antique car show. When the planned Performing Arts Center becomes a reality at the foot of Kentucky Avenue and the Railroad Museum joins the Maritime Center in the same area, downtown Paducah will pulse as never before. The Maiden Alley Theater, which began construction on its new building in October 2000, now offers independent films from around the world at its new location. A lighted marquee spans the alley announcing the new attractions.

The centerpiece of the revival of downtown Paducah is the annual international quilt festival sponsored by the American Quilter's Society, which formed in 1984 and had its first show the following year. This show attracts entries and participants from around the world. The brainchild of William and Meredith Schroeder, the show brought approximately 36,000 to the Paducah area in the year 2000. The Executive Inn and the Convention Center are jammed to the maximum during the event. Showrooms spring up all over the city. Churches open their doors to help feed the influx and rooms are in as great a shortage as when the construction boom hit the Paducah area in the 1950s. In fact, all rooms

Visitors take advantage of the Mary Yeiser Art Center in the market house during the summer of 2001.

First Street to the Executive Inn became a mall during the fall Barbecue Festival in 2001.

Currently, the annual quilt festival brings to Paducah as many visitors as there are residents in the city.

for a 60-mile radius are usually taken. The Paducah show awards handsome prizes ($18,000 for the top quilt in 2000) that totaled $108,000 in 2000 (the highest in the industry). Master and amateur quilters vie for an opportunity to participate in the Paducah show.

The Museum of the American Quilter's Society opened in 1991. It houses a permanent collection of quilts plus traveling exhibits that served 46,000 visitors in 2000. The museum also sponsors workshops and educational events that focus on the art of quilting and its place in the evolution of American culture. Each fall, the site also hosts an exhibit that is growing in popularity. The fifth annual Arts in Action show allows visitors to see arts and crafts that now are all but lost.

Held when the blooms are at their peak, the annual Dogwood Trail Celebration usually coincides with the Quilt Show. Yards and streets throughout Paducah burst into beauty along the 12-mile-long trail. Residents and city workers take special pride in presenting Paducah at its best during the occasion. A continuous line of cars and buses wends its way along the trail each evening during the season in mid-April.

Another draw to downtown Paducah that owes its origins to the Schroeders is the mural project on the floodwall. Artist Robert Dafford continually exceeds the high expectations of the Murals Committee, which has the final say on what goes where and how the marker should read. A concerted effort has been made to assure that each image is both accurate and historically significant. Every panel is the product of community concern. No government funds are involved. The

Robert Dafford, the lead artist on Paducah's mural project, puts the city's history on display on a grand scale.

Visitors to Paducah view the city's history on the murals painted on the floodwalls.

The oldest structure in downtown Paducah is the Louisville Bank, which once also housed Petter Supply. This building has been renovated and is now home to the River Heritage Museum.

scheme from Broadway downriver is chronological and the focus is on major events in the history of the city. From Broadway upriver, the theme is the river industry and its transition into the railroad era in Paducah. To date, the only conflict between the City and the Murals Committee was over the church mural. To avoid any hint of church and state concerns, the committee decided to show the buildings housing church congregations in Paducah prior to 1860. The result is adequate but loses the impact that religion actually had upon the development of the character of the community. Perhaps the old adage that a camel is a horse designed by government decree is apt.

The latest addition to the collage of events is the "Living Mural" presentation by the city Parks and Recreation Department and filmed by the television department of Paducah Community College. Each new mural comes to life briefly as actors explain the significance of the events portrayed. The Paducah Community Band and other musicians also perform. The video appears often on Channel 2, the public access station of Paducah.

A major renovation in the older part of the city was the transformation of the 1843 Federal Bank Building, which once housed Petter Supply, into the River Heritage Museum. The idea arose in 1988 and a board met in 1990. The museum is a private, non-profit educational organization seeking to stimulate interest and awareness in the rivers and their contribution to the local community. The group hopes to rekindle Mark Twain's lust for life on the river: "Your true pilot cares

The American Queen, *part of which is shown here at the foot of Broadway, is the largest tourist boat on the inland waterway. This "monster" has five decks.*

nothing about anything on earth but the river, and his pride in his occupation surpasses the pride of kings."

Paducah's Downtown after Dinner Program offers live music on most corners from Sixth to the river on Saturday evenings between May and October. Crisp fall days bring the tempting smell of barbecue to the riverfront, toots of antique steam engines at Carson Park, and the haunting sound of the pipes at Carson Park announcing the annual Highland Games in early September that celebrate the Celtic culture common to many in the area. The arrival of the *Delta Queen*, the *Mississippi Queen*, or the *American Queen* adds to the festive mood as passengers fan out to enjoy the antique stores, quality restaurants, and museums in the downtown area.

Paducah formed the first Lions Club in Kentucky on April 13, 1920. Over the years this club emerged as a leading fund-raiser for children with handicaps in four states: Illinois, Missouri, Tennessee, and Kentucky. The annual WPSD-TV Telethon of Stars continues to grow. It closed in 2000 with pledges exceeding $525,000. The remarkable thing about this event is that its costs are kept to a minimum and more than 90 percent of funds raised actually go to the various programs to benefit handicapped children. This care for community and for the less fortunate is one of the hallmarks of Paducah over its entire history.

In July 2000, an old institution in downtown Paducah entered a new era. The public library evolved into the McCracken County Public Library. The origins of this institution go back to the religious revivals of the early 1900s. In 1901,

Kentucky's first Lions Club was founded in Paducah; members are shown here in a meeting at the Irvin Cobb Hotel.

A radio auction of the Paducah Lions Club was the precursor to today's "Telethon of Stars." Pictured are Sam Locke and Sam Sloan Sr. (Courtesy MHM.)

the local ministerial association asked Reverend George W. Perryman, pastor of the First Baptist Church, and J.R. Puryear, surveyor of customs at the port of Paducah, to contact Andrew Carnegie, who, by then, had become known as "The Patron Saint of Libraries." Karl Marx, the socialist, felt that religion was "the opiate of the masses," and could be used by the capitalists to keep the working man in subjugation. Carnegie, the capitalist, felt that the opportunity to read was the chance for the working man to improve himself and stay out of trouble at the same time. The City learned that Carnegie would provide funds if the City committed itself to the support of the library. As a result, Carnegie donated $35,000 and the public library in Paducah was born.

Residents of Paducah flocked to the new Carnegie Library on its opening October 4, 1904. The structure designed by A.L. Lassiter, a local architect, was impressive and provided an atmosphere conducive to reading and study. The original collection of 1,800 carefully selected volumes soon had to be expanded. Citizens of Paducah were welcomed but others had to have permission to use the facility. African Americans were relegated to a collection located in the basement. Visitors were admonished that "silence must be observed in the reading rooms. Loud talking, laughing, and other noisy demonstrations are expressly forbidden in the library building. Use of tobacco will not be permitted in any form. Spitting on the floors or any other part of the building is positively prohibited."

The library began to expand in 1926, when the county agreed to contribute to the operating expenses. This initial gesture became reality in 2000. Over the years the library developed into a vital part of the life of Paducah. Additions were made

Paducah received a grant from Andrew Carnegie for the construction of a public library. This facility opened on October 4, 1904, but was destroyed by fire in 1964. (Courtesy McCPL.)

The Carnegie Public Library welcomed native son Irvin S. Cobb in 1911. (Courtesy McCPL.)

and new programs began, but that was not to last. On December 30, 1964, the structure was destroyed by a fire that started among the decorations put up for children in the basement. The building could not be salvaged and the part of the collection that was saved was moved temporarily to the old PJC building next to Broadway Methodist Church.

On April 28, 1970, the Paducah Public Library opened for business. The new structure, designed by Don Peck and Associates of Paducah, was modern, air-conditioned, carpeted, and capable of housing a comprehensive collection of various media, not just books. The site was adjacent to the new City Hall and faced the plaza that connects the City Hall with the County Court House on Washington Street. The library grounds became the province of the Paducah Garden Club while the Little Garden Club saw to the indoor décor. The original 30,000 books grew to more than 100,000 and the availability of media other than print has grown exponentially. But continued growth put a strain on the city, with its declining tax base. In 1999, the board of the library presented a request for a countywide library-taxing district. With this, the library can now look to the next millennium with assurance that funding will be available to provide quality service to the entire area.

The summer of 2000 boded ill for Paducah. Gloom hung over the community as USEC, Inc. (the firm operating the gaseous diffusion plant) pondered whether to close the plant at Paducah or at Portsmouth, Ohio. It was with relief that Paducahans read the article by Joe Walker in the *Paducah Sun* on June 22, 2000, announcing that the axe missed the city. Even so, the number of jobs would be reduced. What the report missed was that the welcomed decision had hidden opportunity costs. Gradually, the fears of some proved to have merit. In the rush to produce uranium during the cold war, long-term contamination had been ignored or down played. Contamination from leakages and spills seems to be responsible for a plethora of health problems for workers and contamination of water and soil in the area promises future headaches to restore the safety of the environment. High-paying jobs helped, but the "spillover" costs are also high. Still, people can watch the boats on the river or kick back at Nobel Park and enjoy life in Paducah for now.

The pond at Noble Park takes on an icy coat late in 2001.

17. Lest We Forget . . .

In "Everyman His Own Historian," Carl Becker observed that each generation must redefine its view of the past. Heroes of previous ages often fall out of favor and new personalities emerge. Over the years, many in Paducah have made significant contributions to their community, to their companions on the road of life, and to their relationship with their maker. Often, these individuals are quiet, unassuming citizens who rise to a challenge that changes the community.

Walter C. Jetton is, to Paducahans, the image of what many remember of Augusta Tilghman High School. His strict approach to discipline still brings shivers to those who ran afoul of his rules. Nevertheless, Jetton is held up as the explanation of why this school achieved national recognition in many areas—academics, athletics, arts, music, and so on. Nostalgia reveals a wish for the return of this approach to education.

In Paducah, R.G. Matheson is "the Dean." Many do not know that was a title, not a given name. Matheson arrived at Paducah Junior College when the two-year college movement was gaining momentum across the nation. The Dean took a leading role in Kentucky. By the 1960s, the University of Kentucky entered the two-year college scene by establishing a community college system. Matheson felt that PJC might be better suited for affiliation with Murray State, which was transforming itself from a regional teacher's college into a regional university at that time. Community pressure mounted and finally, PJC merged with the new system. Matheson was 67 and thus not able to continue as chief administrative officer under the UK rules. He accepted a position as consultant on the accreditation of the new system. As such, he played a major role in the growth, accreditation, and acceptance of the new system and its academic programs.

Matheson died on December 15, 1991, at age 91. The funeral at Paducah's First Presbyterian Church would have pleased him. A large crowd gathered to celebrate his life. The service was solemn, the sermon profound; however, what really would have amused the wry Scot was the fact that it took two hearses to get him to the cemetery. The pallbearers put the Dean in a grand white Cadillac and went to their own vehicles only to be recalled to remove him and place him in another hearse. The battery was dead!

Oscar Cross (1906–1999) was small in stature but his spirit was too large to be confined. He shared it with his community. Almost unnoticed and without outside support, Cross founded the Paducah Boy's Club, primarily for young

LEFT: *Oscar Cross gave tirelessly of himself to promote youth in the inner city.*
RIGHT: *The third winningest coach in the NCAA was Clarence "Big House" Gains, a native of Paducah. (Courtesy Gale Ridgeway.)*

black children who lacked any other facilities at the time, and served as its director for 50 years. He was the first African American to serve as a juvenile officer of McCracken County. He received many awards over the years including the Kentucky Education Association's Lucy Harth Smith-Atwood S. Wilson Award for civil and human rights in education in 1987. In 1993, Cross was the recipient of the Boys and Girls Club Herman S. Prescott Award for individuals who make significant contributions in human rights for minorities and women. Armed with little but faith and dedication, Oscar Cross changed the lives of those youth most vulnerable in his community.

Clarence "Big House" Gains left a segregated Paducah and became a legend in college basketball at Winston Salem State University in North Carolina, ending with a career that compares with Adolph Rupp and other legends.

Claude "Sonny" Haws took his two-year college team to the National Championship in basketball in 1969. Coaching both baseball and basketball, Haws never wavered in affirming that his players were students first and athletes afterward.

Henry "Speedie" Atkins appeared on ABC's *That's Incredible* in 1980 with Mrs. Velma Hamock of Paducah. What is remarkable about this is that Speedie died in 1928. He proved to be a successful example of a still secret process of mummification and became an icon to the community when he floated out of a mortuary in 1937 and was cleaned up with a bit of Tide. No one seemed to object to the bizarre ritual of a parade of elementary school students from near and far passing by the remains of Mr. Atkins. On Friday, August 5, 1994, Speedie finally was lowered into his grave at Maple Lawn cemetery.

Sam Sloan Sr. helped found the first Lions Club in Kentucky. Sloan contributed to almost every community organization and became known locally as "Mr. Paducah." Bill Powell reported in the local paper on November 13, 1960, that Sloan was both secretary and treasurer of six civic organizations at once during the late 1930s. Sloan helped found the Kitty League with professional baseball played at Brooks Stadium. He lived by the adage that to have a friend, one must be a friend.

Paducah's greatest achievement to date is its Lions-WPSD-TV telethon benefiting handicapped children in four states. Over a 44-year period, this annual event raised $16,700,586, with expenses only averaging 11 percent! This production moved to the Executive Inn in 1986 and continued to grow. Dan Steele of WPSD-TV believes that this telethon is the largest in the nation in per-capita giving. Also, it is purely a local Lions Club project. "That is a tribute to the people of this area, because it is only their support of the disabled that has allowed the Lions and WPSD-TV to continue one of television's longest-running annual shows."

Paducah continues to recreate itself. Each generation adds to its institutions and memories. Somehow the city finds a way of overcoming obstacles and retaining its optimism. The youths of one era mellow into the leaders of the next, winnowing and sifting, changing and transforming continually to retain the essence of the city.

Claude "Sonny" Haws (lower left) won the national championship in two-year college basketball in 1969 while at Paducah Junior College. (Courtesy The Arrowhead, *PCC.)*

Appendix
The Mayors of Paducah

Jesse H. Gardner, 1857–1859

John W. Sauner, 1859–1863

John G. Fisher, 1863–1865

John W. Sauner, 1867–1871

Meyer Weil, 1871–1875

John G. Fisher, 1875–1877

Meyer Weil, 1877–1881

Charles Reed, 1881–1889

Joseph H. Johnson, 1889–1891

David M. Yeiser Sr., 1891–1897

James M. Lang, 1897–1901

David A. Yeiser Sr., 1901–1908

James P. Smith, 1908–1912

Thoms N. Hazelip, 1912–1916

Ernest Lackey, 1916 (election voided)

Frank N. Burns, 1916–1920

F.W. Katterjohn, 1920–1924

J.N. Bailey, 1924–1928

Ernest Lackey, 1928–1932

Ed G. Scott, 1932–1936

Edgar T. Washburn, 1936–1940

Pierce Lackey, 1940–1944

Wayne C. Seaton, 1944–1948

Gene Peak, 1948 (died)

Stewart Johnson, 1949–1952

Robert C. Cherry, 1952–1956

George Jacobs, 1956–1960

Robert C. Cherry, 1960–1964

Tom Wilson, 1964–1968

Robert C. Cherry, 1968–1972

Mrs. Houston McNutt, 1972–1976

William S. Murphy, 1976–1980

John Penrod, 1980–1984

Joe Viterisi, 1984–1988

Geraldine Montgomery, 1988–1996

Albert Jones, 1996–2001

William Paxton, 2001 to present

BIBLIOGRAPHY

American Annual Cyclopaedia and Register of Important Facts, 1861. New York: D. Appleton and Co., 1865.

Battle, J.H., W.H. Perrin, and G.C. Kniffin. *Kentucky: A History of the State*. Louisville, KY: F.A. Battey Publishing Co., 1885.

Black, William R. III. *A History of Race Relations in the Paducah Schools*. Princeton, NJ: unpublished thesis, 1996.

Blythe, Janett Marie. *A Pictorial History of a School*. Paducah: Turner Publishing, 2000.

Clark, Thomas D. *A History of Kentucky*. Lexington, KY: The John Bradford Press, 1960.

Collins, Richard H. *History of Kentucky*. Frankfort: Kentucky Historical Society, 1966.

Corliss, Carlton J. *Main Line of Mid-America*. New York: Creative Gae Press, 1950.

Coulter, Ellis Merton. *The Civil War and Reconstruction in Kentucky*. Chapel Hill: The University of North Carolina Press, 1926.

Cunningham, Bill. *On Bended Knee*. Nashville: McClanahan Press, 1983.

Deupree, J.G. *The Noxubee Squadron of the First Mississippi Cavalry, C.S.A., 1861–1865*. Jackson: Mississippi Historical Society, 1918.

Fairhurst, Richard E. *The Fairhurst Essays: A Public Look at a Private Memoir*. Gerard, MO: The Patrice Press, 1980.

Franklin, John Hope. *From Slavery to Freedom: A History of Negro Americans*. New York: Alfred A. Knopf, 1974.

Grant, Ulysses S. *Personal Memoirs*. New York: Charles L. Webster and Co., 1885.

Jewell, Virginia. *Lick Skillet and Other Tales of Hickman County*. Union City, TN: Lanzer Printing Co., 1986.

Kaufman, Max. *Tales from Specks of Dust: Poems of the Atomic Age*. New York: The William-Frederick Press, 1947.

Langstaff, George Quigley, ed. *Quintus Quincy Quigley, The Life and Times of Quintus Quincy Quigley, 1828–1910: His Personal Journal*. Nashville: Tallent Communications Group, 1999.

Miller, John G. *The Black Patch War*. Chapel Hill: The University of North Carolina Press, 1936.

Mofield, William Ray. *The Atomic Age Comes to Paducah*. Columbia University: unpublished thesis, 1957.

Robertson, John E.L. *Paducah, 1830–1980, a Sesquicentennial History*. Paducah: Image Graphics, 1980.

———. *Paducah: A Pictorial History*. St. Louis: G. Bradley Publishing, 1988.

———. *The History of Citizens Bank: 100th Anniversary*. Paducah: Image Graphics, 1988.

Robertson, John E.L., and Margaret Robertson. *Fountain Avenue United Methodist Church: A Centennial History*. Paducah: Image Graphics, 1992.

Sandburg, Carl. *Abraham Lincoln: The Prairie Years and the War Years*. Pleasantville, NY: Reader's Digest, 1970.

Shannon, Jasper B., and Ruth McQuown. *Presidential Politics in Kentucky, 1824–1948*. Lexington: University of Kentucky Press, 1950.

Stover, John F. *History of the Illinois Central Railroad*. New York: McMillan Publishing Co.

Thompson, H.E. *Paducah Historically*. Paducah: Young Printing, 1910.

War of the Rebellion: Official Records of the Union and Confederate Armies. Washington, D.C.: Government Printing Office, 1871.

Williams, ?. *Paducah Directory, City Guide and Business Mirror*. Paducah: Bryan and Clements, 1859.

Extensive use of newspapers back to the Civil War was possible due to the collections of the McCracken County Public Library, the Filson Club, Murray State University, the University of Kentucky, and the University of Louisville Libraries.

Tape-recorded interviews with various mayors and members of the city commission provided the basis for the section on recent politics, and interviews with survivors of the 1937 flood provided the basis for that section.

Public sources include census documents, the *Acts of Kentucky, Kentucky Senate and House Journals*, and city and county order books.

The Meriwether Lewis Clark papers in the Clark Family Collection of the Missouri Historical Society in St. Louis cleared up the issue of the naming of Paducah. The George Goodman Papers at the University of Kentucky deal with the WPA in Kentucky, the Harvey papers on integration are from the files of Reverend Harvey in Paducah, and the papers of Andrew Jackson in the Library of Congress gave insight to the treaty ceding the "Purchase" from the Chickasaw to the United States.

INDEX

The Kentucky Visitor Center at Whitehaven welcomes travelers on I-24 and U.S. 45 to Paducah. This structure almost fell to the wreckers but was saved by Governor John Y. Brown and dedicated preservationists such as Bill Black. Memorabilia of Alben Barkley occupies the second floor.